The Quiet Sense

How I know that God is real

By
Karen Sinclair

THE QUIET SENSE

The Quiet Sense

How I know that God is real

By
KAREN SINCLAIR

THE QUIET SENSE

THE QUIET SENSE

Published by Karen Sinclair
Print Edition

Copyright © 2017 Karen Sinclair
All Rights Reserved

UNITED STATES COPYRIGHT OFFICE REGISTRATION NUMBER
TXu 2-021-093
ISBN 978-09814505-3-7

CATALOGUING DATA

Sinclair, Karen
THE QUIET SENSE: How I know that God is real
Summary: Analysis of Christian spiritual life, beliefs, faith and disillusionment.

1. Christian Faith   2. Christian Beliefs   3. Unbelief   4. Disillusionment

PERMISSIONS

THE HOLY BIBLE, NEW INTERNATIONAL VERSION®, NIV® COPYRIGHT © 1973, 1978, 1984, 2011 BY BIBLICA, INC.® USED BY PERMISSION. ALL RIGHTS RESERVED WORLDWIDE.

HOLY BIBLE, NEW INTERNATIONAL VERSION® ANGLICIZED, NIV® COPYRIGHT © 1979, 1984, 2011 BY BIBLICA, INC.® USED BY PERMISSION. ALL RIGHTS RESERVED WORLDWIDE.

THE 21ST CENTURY KING JAMES VERSION®, COPYRIGHT © 1994. USED BY PERMISSION OF DEUEL ENTERPRISES, INC., GARY, SD 57237. ALL RIGHTS RESERVED

SCRIPTURE QUOTATIONS MARKED (NLT) ARE TAKEN FROM THE HOLY BIBLE, NEW LIVING TRANSLATION, COPYRIGHT © 1996, 2004, 2007 BY TYNDALE HOUSE FOUNDATION. USED BY PERMISSION OF TYNDALE HOUSE PUBLISHERS, INC., CAROL STREAM, ILLINOIS 60188. ALL RIGHTS RESERVED.

THE HOLY BIBLE: INTERNATIONAL STANDARD VERSION. RELEASE 2.0, BUILD 2015.02.09. COPYRIGHT © 1995-2014 BY ISV FOUNDATION. ALL RIGHTS RESERVED INTERNATIONALLY. USED BY PERMISSION OF DAVIDSON PRESS, LLC.

Editor: Joanne Sher
Cover Font: THE QUIET SENSE by Seth Martin
Printed by CreateSpace, An Amazon.com Company

THE QUIET SENSE

KAREN SINCLAIR
P.O. BOX 206
SOUTH ORANGE, NJ 07079
UNITED STATES OF AMERICA

WWW.KARENSWALL.COM

THE QUIET SENSE

Table of Contents

S
Dedication xi
Acknowledgments xii
Preface xiv
Introduction xvi
PART I 1
LENS OF THE QUIET SENSE 1
   Chapter 1: Eternal Life in Perspective 2
   Chapter 2: Theories, Perspectives & Realities of Life 20
      Perspectives of Life 20
      Beliefs from the Bible 24
      Belief in the Theory of Evolution 34
   Chapter 3: Life Well Lived 44
      Plentiful Dimensions 46
      Physical Life 47
      The Exponential Human Mind 49
      Spirited Life 51
   Chapter 4: The Kingdom of Heaven 61
      Clues to the Kingdom 63
      Many Mansions 70
      Paradise Found 71
   Chapter 5: Unanswered Prayer 78
   Chapter 6: Darkly Though a Looking Glass- Poor Eve 92
   Chapter 7: Dimensions of Truth 104

Scribes, Journalists and other Messengers 104

Inspired Texts 106

Truths of Science and Theory 107

Chapter 8: Essential Truth 113

PART II 124

AWAKENING THE QUIET SENSE 124

Chapter 9: Exposing Misunderstandings 125

Illness-free Life 126

Death Penalty 127

Misperceived Limit of God's Power 130

Self-healing Body 133

Secularity in Celebrations 134

A Few Good Worshippers 136

A Hierarchy of Christians 140

Chapter 10: Under the Stand of Faith 145

On Gifted Wings 149

Faith Without Works 154

Chapter 11: Boundaries of Belief 160

What is Belief? 160

The Belief that Jesus was sent by God 162

Belief in One God 163

Belief in The Son 167

Belief in Salvation 168

Chapter 12: The Mystique of Christian Connectedness 176

A Rounded Perspective of Prayer 176

Communion of Saints 187

Giving from the Spirit 190

Chapter 13: Jokes and Taunts that Go "Boom" in the Light 203

Chapter 14: Things Hoped For 213

The Resurrection of the Body 213

Life Everlasting 214

Paradise 215

Era of Purpose 216

In God's Hands 217

Hope of Love 219

Forgiveness- The Promise 220

The Second Coming 222

World Without End 225

Conclusions 228

References 234

S

Dedication

This book is lovingly dedicated to my parents May and Ovid Blackman whose nurturing gifts to me I am only aware of with hindsight, and to the poor in spirit who inspired this urge to communicate the quiet truth that makes me strong. In short this is dedicated to those who nurture and those wanting to receive the gift of knowing without a doubt that God is real.

Acknowledgments

Businesses and individuals whose principles of social responsibility make access to information and services universally available are a major hidden input in the research and production of this book. I would specifically cite Google, Biblegateway.com, Theopedia.com and West Orange Public Library. Universal availability of resources is an important research pillar.

I must also thank my editor, Joanne Sher, a faith writer and editor, whose task it was to read my freshly spawned analyses and help me bring the message in this book to those eager to discover how I know that God exists.

I became ill after I started this book and a team of medical specialists helped take care of the disease. Most of the time I was able to continue researching and writing. Completion of this book therefore bears a debt to the medical help I received as well as to encouragement from family and friends.

Finally, I am grateful to my sisters Paula and Janis who patiently shared this journey with me. Most of all, I thank God for inspiring my thoughts, sustaining my health; for innumerable resources to continue to research, analyze and write, and for the loving evidence of the Body of Christ in support of this humble part. I experienced many miracles and can confirm that it was all one, and that God's Grace is sufficient for me.

Preface

We owe the understanding that humans have five senses to renowned philosopher Aristotle, who lived 380 years before Christ. That understanding prevailed for centuries, is what I learned in school, and is what many today accept. Yet this understanding co-exists with the clear acknowledgment of other obvious senses such as the sense of balance (equilibrium) that keeps us stable and the indisputable senses of hunger and thirst. Indeed, psychologists and neurologists studying human sensory systems have consensus on at least twenty-one senses.

Doubt in God's existence can function similarly. The experience of God is not a conscious encounter based on our formal education. The idea of God simply does not fit in to the science we are taught, and our education offers little vocabulary to define the experience of God's presence.

Many believe that, for example, understanding the development of a fetus, the process of cloning, genetic alteration, and manipulation of living cells make life a matter of science and therefore antithetical to God. In that regard, our education prepares us to recognize experiences and define concepts as diverse as gravity, weather, DNA and chemical reactions as scientific, but does not prepare us to recognize God.

It is more popular in our culture to ignore things that we do not understand, to dismiss inexplicable dreams and nameless sensations and to overlook various subsets of our experiences, so they can correspond with contemporary definitions of reality. Customarily, the mystery of dreams, sleep, and death fall prey to this practice, as does the mystery of God. Embracing science as superior, educators often substitute descriptive analyses of life for understanding, and equate observer with architect and observation with science rather than God.

This book is an attempt to recognize and acknowledge evidence of God, dispel some commonly held myths and explain why some truths in the Bible appear to educated minds to be artifice. In the process, the book heightens awareness of the sense of God: The Quiet Sense. It is a mammoth task to attempt to share this knowledge in a world that recognizes five senses. I cannot unravel over two thousand years of Aristotle's wisdom in one book. Instead, this book attempts to awaken individual recognition of God. It uses contemporary understanding and vocabulary to point to the truth beyond the reality we circumscribe by our perceptions of time and things. So help me, God.

Introduction

Some aspects of Christianity loom as major obstacles to belief. Misunderstanding may also encourage disbelief or serve as a prop for desperate people seeking any solution for their distressing reality. Desperation can foster vulnerability to exploitation and hollow promises of misguided leaders.

The New Testament warns us to beware of false prophets. (Matthew 7:15) But the quandary is how to recognize them. Some snares raise red flags to the wary and reinforce barriers that keep thinking, reasoning people from God. Skeptics cite the red flags—any theft, dishonest priest, church scandal, deception, financial scandal, money making scheme, and the like -- not merely as human flaws, but as black marks against the church, faith and, most profoundly, the truth of God's existence.

Understanding why I know (not just believe, not merely think) that God is real requires explanations of my perspectives of the Bible, its major principles and convictions, concepts of faith and hope, rituals and even the impact of violations by Christian leaders, and of course life and death.

Part I explores relevant aspects of my perspective. Recognizing that everyone's story is not mine, Part II expands the discussion to cross other hurdles and adjust the viewing lens to other perspectives. Chapter by chapter, this book addresses particular concepts that may be stumbling blocks to reasoning, thinking people and snares to the gullible. Concepts of eternal life, death, faith, creation, the mystique of Christian connectedness, concerns about public ridicule, thorns and snares are analyzed with reason. What is faith if it is shaken by a question?

This book is expected to encourage the reader to expand on the author's insight. Questions to reflect and explore at the end of each chapter attempt to promote frank discussion, unearth misgivings, and encourage readers to face an expanded scope of matters related to awakening the Quiet Sense. They may be helpful for study by Christians and skeptics alike and can open dialogue about concepts in contemporary contexts. Tolerance and respect of both believers and skeptics are maintained throughout these discussions and it is hoped that readers will face the quest with similar attitudes.

Teachings in the entire Bible cannot be addressed in one book. This book positions the Bible among the array of elements in modern life and clarifies its relevance. Open-minded analysis repeatedly shifts between Bible analogies with vines, sheep, lamps and ancient concerns, and analogies with modern computers, cell phones and possessions more accessible to modern reader. The Quiet Sense encourages fearless discussion of the mysteries of selected Christian beliefs in the context of contemporary skepticism and unbelief. It would be my delight if after reading the selected perspectives, you can see (and hopefully share) *how I KNOW that God is real.*

PART I

LENS OF THE QUIET SENSE

See to it that no one takes you captive through hollow and deceptive philosophy, which depends on human tradition and the basic principles of this world rather than on Christ.
  Colossians 2:8 (NIVUK)

Chapter 1: Eternal Life in Perspective

Christians can sometimes misunderstand the concept of eternal life. I am a Christian and I believe in eternal life. Before we begin to discuss this, I must clarify this indisputable truth:

We are all going to die.

I believe this, even though I believe in eternal life. Christians who tell you that if you toe the Christian line you are going to live forever do not understand eternal life. Similarly, being told to stop eating meat, give up dancing, abstain from sex, suffer, endure insults from non-believers, give all your money to the church, tithe, feed the poor, give your body to be burned for salvation completely misrepresent eternal life and the meaning of some of the writings in the Bible. Some accounts in the Bible relate incidents that occurred; others are metaphorical. Taken together, they shape the truth presented in the Bible. Eternal life does not mean that your body is never going to die.

This is not a fatalistic discussion, but a realist perspective that offers comfort in the truth instead of through delusion and inane platitude. Even those who were once raised from the dead are no longer physically present with us. The only historic exception is Christ, who lives on earth today through people (see explanation of the Body of Christ in the section "Communion of Saints" in Chapter 12: The Mystique of Christian Connectedness). For us, the only exception will be if the second coming (discussed in Chapter 14: Things Hoped For) should precede our death.

I can't say when, but I can say that this understanding is one of the basic foundations of this discussion. If you've ever gone to a funeral, you can take the realist perspective as we talk of eternal life: however much you do, death will be yours also. We are alive now, but death is inevitable for each of us... in some, yet unknown, one of our tomorrows.

King Solomon concluded after all his royal accomplishments, flamboyant experiences and self-indulgences that despite grandeur or meagerness, our lives share essentially a common destiny. In his writings in the Bible, he concluded:

> *this is your lot in life and in your toilsome labor under the sun. Whatever your hand finds to do, do it with all your might, for in the realm of the dead, where you are going, there is neither working nor planning nor knowledge nor wisdom.*
>
> *Ecclesiastes 9:9-10 (NIV)*

This truth is even more pithily expressed in the New Testament, acknowledging death together with the promise of eternal life:

> *For as in Adam all die, so in Christ all will be made alive.*

1 Corinthians 15:22 (NIV)

When I was about nine or ten years old, I had my first experience facing the death of a child. One of my school mates, who had just the previous semester moved on to the most prestigious high school in my community, died. I was told that my former schoolmate Jenny Noms (name changed for privacy of the family) had died of leukemia. Child that I was, it was hard to digest. Only months younger than Jenny, I was coming right behind her, hoping also to earn a place in that elite high school. At that immature age, I could not fathom that she could have died after attaining an accomplishment that, at that age, seemed to me to be the epitome of stardom. I could not comprehend it. There was no grief counseling in school as there is in many American schools today, so I took my confusion home. *What was leukemia? How could she die?* My mother answered all my questions as truthfully as she could and one of the life-changing things she told me was that we were all going to die someday.

I was speechless! I don't know if my mother knew how much time I spent after that revelation closing my eyes and trying to imagine death. I tried to remember whenever I looked at her, at my father, at my sisters, at everyone I met, that they were all going to die someday. I could not put into words the confusion I was experiencing, and looking back, I imagine no one knew how this affected me and for how long.

The thing that struck me then was that everyone seemed to be moving merrily along. My mother was also so matter-of-fact about it that I was not scared, just completely stunned. Being the youngest in my family, I had become accustomed to learning seemingly new things that everyone else in the world already knew. So I spent time getting accustomed to the reality of human death: looking at things, then closing my eyes and imagining that I couldn't see them anymore. After all, one day, I was going to die.

After a while, having closed and opened my eyes in enough death imaginings, I resolved that this was merely something new that I had to come to terms with, like learning about traffic signs, currency and the correct way to brush my teeth. I reasoned that since everyone else already knew and yet they were moving along with life, I needed to follow their example and just keep going. From then on, everything I learned was taken matter-of-factly within the context of death.

I understood Christ's message about eternal life within the context of the reality of death. I never met my mother's parents. My maternal grandparents had died when my mother was a teenager. By the time I came along, they were ancient news. They were the cast of fascinating stories of outmoded travels, trains, telegrams, stand pipes, Tilly lamps, cows with names and country life of a time far off. It was as if they had *always* been dead. The one grandmother I knew, my father's mother, had not yet died. But she seemed too ancient to die. In my childish perspective, it seemed to me then that it was little children – children like my former schoolmate - who were most vulnerable. It did not escape me that I was much like her.

I came to grips with the truth of my mortality at about age ten. Once you accept that you are going to die, time and things take on a different meaning and the context of your life and other truths you encounter include that knowledge. Although I can still today remember my schoolmate lying in her coffin in her pink nightdress, after a while, I was not afraid, but alert to those things that gave life. I share all this so that you also will not build your faith by denying any of the realities of your life.

The message that Christ came to tell us is NOT that we would never lose the lives we are living. Matthew 5:17, Luke 4:18 and 1 Timothy 1:15 teach us that Christ came to fulfill the laws of this life that we know and to save us from its pitfalls of this life: Pitfalls that affect the Kingdom of God. Paul expressed this pithily:

> *...Christ Jesus came into the world to save sinners of whom I am the worst.*

1 Timothy 1:15 (NIV)

While Jesus came to proclaim good news, free, heal and set the oppressed free, (Luke 4:18) the reason behind all this, -- his mission -- was to ensure us the path to salvation. In this regard, he said:

the son of man came to seek and to save the lost.

Luke 19:10 (NIV)

Christ's mission and purpose are the kind of butterfly message that a caterpillar would find hard to understand as it pursues its crawling, munching, sedentary life experience. It is the kind of message that would bemuse an unborn baby swimming alone in a womb completely circumscribed in the safety of his mother's body; comforted and nurtured effortlessly by her efforts and through her invisible (at least to him) world. Imagine having to tell that baby about our world. How could one tell of another life of walking, talking, making music: a life containing millions of other people, colorful flowers, fresh air, and space wider than the world of the womb? What about a chicken and its egg? How would you explain to a little chick, rolling around in his own shell, that one day he would be free of the confines of that fragile horizon? Unbelievable! Incomprehensible!

It would be hard to tell the caterpillar, the unborn baby, the un-hatched chicken, that when they lose the life they have, they will be transformed to begin experience in a completely different form. The very concepts of life for the unborn chick and baby are completely different from the realities of the world they enter after birth. Both the concepts and the realities know no parallel in their unborn status. So too it is with the journey of human life through to death. What happens next is as unlike our world as our world is to the unborn baby in a womb; the unborn chick in an eggshell; the sedentary caterpillar riveted on a branch. That is similar to the context of Christ's message. Christ explained to us what would happen to our lives after we died, when we thought of life only in the form that preceded death. Death is the destiny of the body.

We may not fully understand what it means that the Spirit gives birth to spirit. It is difficult even to talk about a life beyond the one we experience. Our vocabulary comes from our existing life and shared world experiences. Our civilization developed our way to measure time, physical growth, and space, and name objects we encounter. We name the animals and trees we see and pronounce names on newborn babies. We describe feelings, pain, love and ideas including ideas of God and concepts of belief, hope and time. We represent our interpretations of time in numbered clocks and updated almanacs, yet there is no vocabulary to talk about the concepts beyond physical life. We just don't know them well enough.

Like the caterpillar, we can hardly think of such a life, much less *believe*.

Our belief is couched in understanding. We understand the concept of "mother" and we trust, without any recollection of it, that we were indeed little swimmers in a womb. Without any specific evidence of this, we believe that we have been given correct information of our mother. We also trust that sperm was involved, that we have a male parent, and in many cases, we actually know our biological father. Without going to med school and studying reproduction ourselves, we understand the concept of father, and there is no doubt that sperm from some man was involved in the process.

The point is, human society is a sharing and handing down of information. Some things in life we can only be told. There is no way to remember everything about our origins. Through oral traditions, many of us understand who our parents and grandparents are. With technical developments over the years, we have photographs and family trees and we are told about our histories and our ancestors. Some things we experience firsthand, but others we learn from others. Christ taught using analogy and metaphor, because our eyes and ears do not perceive what he wanted to share. He specifically explained:

This is why I speak to them in parables:

> *"Though seeing, they do not see;*
> *though hearing, they do not hear or understand.*
> *In them is fulfilled the prophecy of Isaiah:*
> *"'You will be ever hearing but never understanding;*
> *you will be ever seeing but never perceiving.*
> *For this people's heart has become calloused;*
> *they hardly hear with their ears, and they have closed their eyes.*
> *Otherwise they might see with their eyes, hear with their ears,*
> *understand with their hearts and turn, and I would heal them...*
> *Matthew 13:13-15 (NIV)*

I grew up in a warm country and had never seen snow. Everything I knew about snow was based on secondhand information. I listened to descriptions of its coldness and wetness and saw photographs, mainly at Christmas. It was described using similes such as: it is *like* powder or it fell from the sky *like* raindrops or that it was cold *like* ice. We decorated our Christmas trees with cotton balls to look like snow and created little city scenes using crumpled white cloth snow. So too is the talk about another life. Just as cotton balls on a Christmas tree fall short of representing snow, our seeing and hearing can hardly perceive all the dimensions of Christ's message. Without experiencing another life, those who strive to tell us can only use metaphors and parables that relate to those things we already experience.

When I eventually encountered snow, there was more to it than I had been told, yet what I had been told was true. Snow does fall somewhat like raindrops, feels cold like ice, and can be powdery. I learned that it also piles up relentlessly, may be treacherous to walk in, can be melted using salt and cat litter and causes my lips to crack. That's not all; it can have a social dimension in some neighborhoods, as it may be the only time neighbors are outside at the same time, doing the same thing--- scraping ice off the windshields of their cars, shoveling snow from their driveways, lamenting yet another snowfall or blizzard. Though a far cry from cotton balls on a Christmas tree, the cotton balls were not *wrong*, just incomplete. They represented only white fluff perceived by the eye.

Indeed, although I did have an idea about what snow would be like and was prepared for it with all the gear I needed, I only learned what a snow angel was when I got here. I knew enough beforehand so that I would be prepared, even though the experience was grander and much more complex than I had known. I knew to wear boots and a coat. I was prepared enough. As outlined in Matthew 13:8 we can expect that the fertile mind will similarly be prepared to reap the bounty of Christ's message. Recalling the pronouncement about the human spirit:

> *Flesh gives birth to flesh, but the Spirit gives birth to spirit*
>
> *John 3:6 (NIV)*

We are apprised of another life, another birth emerging from the Spirit. One may ask why we need to know about this other life if we will get there through inevitable death. My perception is that not every life blossoms. In this vein, some peas never bloom, some eggs never hatch, some fetuses never develop and some caterpillars somehow do not transform into the beautiful flying spectacle we enjoy fluttering through our gardens. So too can human life fail to attain its full treasure. In words of the Bible:

> *"A farmer went out to sow his seed. As he was scattering the seed, some fell along the path, and the birds came and ate it up. Some fell on rocky places, where it did not have much soil. It sprang up quickly, because the soil was shallow. But when the sun came up, the plants were scorched, and they withered because they had no root. Other seed fell among thorns, which grew up and choked the plants. Still other seed fell on good soil, where it produced a crop—a hundred, sixty or thirty times what was sown. Whoever has ears, let them hear."*
>
> *Matthew 13:3-9 (NIV)*

This reflects the reality we know, that not every life blossoms: some never grow, some are too poorly nurtured to survive, others are destroyed by the "scorching" and "choking" of encounters with life. Christ himself explains:

When anyone hears the message about the kingdom and does not understand it, the evil one comes and snatches away what was sown in their heart. ... But the seed falling on good soil refers to someone who hears the word and understands it. This is the one who produces a crop, yielding a hundred, sixty or thirty times what was sown

Matthew 13:18 & 23 (NIV)

With this information, rather than undertake the impossible task of describing another life, I will focus on helping you to understand my belief that it exists and to comprehend the difficulty of describing it. Belief or unbelief is yours. Obviously, I have not been there and cannot present a first-hand account. I can only share what I perceive based on my understanding and the Holy Spirit's guidance. I want to put into words what I perceive so that I can share with you what I believe is vital.

Nothing I have said so far *proves* anything about origins. Instead, it is evidence that individual life inevitably includes death: when our bodies stop the walking, talking, eating, promiscuous or pious, gay or straight, glamorous or drab, wealthy or deficient, drunken, laughing, dancing or praying lives we know. We use the term "death" to refer to the end of those experiences. Whether we lived in a mansion, a closet or on the sidewalks of a rundown neighborhood; whether we had servants, diamonds and bestselling records, or we were imprisoned, enslaved or free and vagrant; whether we've had breast implants, face lifts, tummy tucks or sex change operations: it makes no difference to death. However much we care for our hair, our teeth or our nails, the day will come when we will die. Everything you understand needs to take that into account.

In the context of that physical death, the message of eternal life that Christ came to earth to tell us about requires us to acknowledge that we are more than meets the eye. Some people acknowledge that as the feeling that no one sees the person that they really are. Some express a certainty that there is a person "inside" waiting to burst out. More eloquently, the poet Paul Laurence Dunbar in his poem "We Wear the Mask" depicted the outer self as a mask worn by the real person inside it:

> *We wear the mask that grins and lies,*
> *It hides our cheeks and shades our eyes, —*
> *This debt we pay to human guile;*
> *With torn and bleeding hearts, we smile,*
> *And mouth with myriad subtleties.*
>
> *Excerpt from the poem "We Wear the Mask" by Paul Laurence Dunbar*
>
> *(1872-1906)*

This poem captures the experience of black people whose bodies were enslaved, but who nevertheless ultimately triumphed over their physical enslavement. After being freed, they emerged whole of spirit and mentally strong. Today many descendants of slaves are phenomenal sources of world music and art, mechanical and scientific discoveries and medical breakthroughs. They display dominance and superiority in sports, endurance and in the execution of strategies of success and skill. In other words, the atrocities of slavery did not obliterate the spirit of the enslaved people. This describes evidence of the separation of body and spirit and the possibility of each pursuing separate lives. It provides a shared perspective for us to embrace the existence of body and spirit.

This is not to suggest that some enslaved people were not broken. Not at all. The point here is that survival is more than a physical accomplishment. Humanity thrives in many planes. Our life is more than physical, even though the physical plane captures our attention most and is most studied, documented, acknowledged and recognized. Christ came to make us aware that, in the context of our physical doings, we also have/ are spiritual beings. To be is not the same as to do. This perspective is confirmed on a massive scale by the evidence of survivors of atrocities of black slavery and the Jewish Holocaust. Again, we can confirm with shared evidence:

Flesh gives birth to flesh, but the Spirit gives birth to spirit
        John 3:6 (NIV)

Though the destination of our bodies is the grave, we have real evidence that our spirit is capable of sustaining beyond the insurmountable challenges of physical life and giving us a new life.

Humans can forget and we each can hardly perceive our own yesterdays with clarity. Our ancestors wanted us to know about them and to document their existence. When I read the first book of the Bible, I become aware of the attempt to document ancestry and of how unwieldy it is. It is mind boggling to think of who begat whom just a few centuries ago, much less so if we try to think of the genesis of the people of the world. When was the beginning? Our ancestors have tried to leave records to help us: records that take us as far back to the "beginning" as is possible. Stories about the beginning have been passed on to us. Just as you wouldn't know where you came from or who your parents were unless someone told you, so too would our ancestors. We have the obligation to tell our children so that information of our origins is passed on and there is no mistake about the origin of the human family.

Recognizing the limitations of my own memory and those of my parents and our dependency on records bequeathed, I read the Bible as handed down documentation. Our ancestors were diligent century after century in passing on vital information to help us overcome and survive. We are not surprised by changes in weather; we predict seasons, build increasingly sophisticated dwellings and pass on intricate mathematical understanding. There is a quiet, invisible dimension masked by our bodies that must also not be forgotten. Using historical documentation, we must also remember where the human race came from, who we are in both body and spirit and where we are going.

Years ago, in my first job after high school, I was working in a data processing center that used a punch card system that was state-of-the-art in that day. I was responsible for one step: collating punch cards in a particular sequence in a chain of steps that involved other people and other machines. After I had mastered my task, I asked my supervisor why it was done that way when there was a more logical sequence. His answer was along the line of, "That is how it has always been done." So, of course, the next day, teenager that I was, I changed my collating sequence to improve my process. Needless to say, all the subsequent processes failed. They had been programmed to expect data collated in one particular sequence. My supervisor had not explained to me the relationship with the processes to follow.

When we cannot perceive the full picture of life, we can hardly prepare without guidance for the processes that are to follow. Wisdom within our professional expertise does not discredit the wisdom of the ages. One applies to the tasks of the life you see, the other addresses the life you cannot yet see.

The Bible describes the (unseen) inner person as the Spirit of Truth:

> *He will give you another Helper ... The Spirit of Truth, whom the world cannot receive, because it neither sees Him nor knows Him;*
>
> *John 14:16-17 (NKJV)*

The spirit is a helper in this life. Acknowledging our spirit is a step in the direction of understanding who we are and of decoding the mysteries of life and death. Understanding the promise of eternal life involves recognizing the body as a vessel, or a mask as Dunbar described. The more we concede to the spirit, the more aware we become that what happens to the body is independent of what happens to the spirit. Then we begin to perceive for ourselves life lived beyond the body and its death. Not only did Christ say:

> *The Spirit gives life;*
>
> *John 6:63 (NIV)*

But he also said:

> *Now this is eternal life: that they know you, the only true God, and Jesus Christ, whom you have sent.*
>
> *John 17:3 (NIV)*

In essence, the experience of eternal life consists of knowing God and Jesus Christ. This understanding of body and spirit is a foundation for discussing truths about life in the next chapter and subsequent ones.

Reflect and Explore:

A) Have you had any experience or encounter with the "mask" described by poet Paul Laurence Dunbar?

B) What struck you most in this chapter's discussion about eternal life?

C) This chapter refers to platitudes. Review some of the things you have heard people say to explain death.

D) When did you first learn that you were going to die? How did and does this information affect you?

Chapter 2: Theories, Perspectives & Realities of Life

Perspectives of Life

I asked Google the question 'What is life?' and received this primary response:

"1. The condition that distinguishes animals and plants from inorganic matter, including the capacity for growth, reproduction, functional activity, and continual change preceding death.

2. The existence of an individual human being or animal.

3. The period between the birth and death of a living thing, especially a human being.

4. (in art) The depiction of a subject from a real model, rather than from an artist's imagination."

Secondary responses from Google referred me to a science text written in 1944 and to cellular and metabolic explanations, including presentations about DNA. There were opportunities to explore discussions about the mechanics of living organisms and the function and operation of organs and processes that maintain life. Life is often equated with those mechanics and processes.

However, life is more than a clump of proteins or sequence of DNA, even though those may be components of your body. Life is an animated experience. Even celebrated scientists who brilliantly dissect, inspect and deduce describe the operation of the intricate nervous system, vital organs and other mysteries of the body often confuse the mechanics of life with life itself. Computer programmers, who painstakingly write line by line of code, understand a truth that users of programs or apps do not: that even features that seem intuitive did not arise by a sudden magical explosion. Instead, each had to be designed and written in, each component assembled, shaped, tested and carefully fitted. Someone made it that way. Every pixel of your screen is programmed. Similarly, while it is commendable that science can sequence millions of human genomes today and even create clones, robots, bio-engineered organs and tissue, the source of life remains a separate subject from the subject of how it is comprised and mechanics of its growth, "operation" and demise. Where did the patterns come from? In that sense, to see God, we distinguish between that 'how' and its operational responses and the mystery of 'How come?' which leads us to 'who?' and questions about origins.

In presenting a twenty-first century perspective of life, DNA Scientist Craig Venter in his presentation titled "What is Life? A 21st Century Perspective", offered the explanation that

"Life is a process of dynamic renewal." That brilliant statement opens an educational feast for a hungry scientific audience. Despite all its inspiration for science, however, it is a descriptive statement that does not reveal how come.

I value the development and advancements that we enjoy in our lives through new understanding, discoveries and scientific study and processes. They are precious. I embrace the discoveries and participate in the advances that are brought to the world. We each have our roles. This is not a book about science. The wealth of scientific knowledge is much better developed, structured and available than is spiritual knowledge, the knowledge of God and the presence of the unexplored senses. My role is to help to uncover them and help show that the body is not all there is to our lives.

Baby boomers have had front row seats to the advancement of computer systems from plodding machines since Charles Babbage's early models were upgraded for popular use in the mid-nineties, and can testify as witnesses to the conversion of silicon into sophisticated processors. Without witnesses who can demonstrate that silicon used in that process is derived from ordinary sand, who would believe that when looking at a microchip? Sand? Some truths are not self-evident. The wisdom from Genesis is that:

God formed a man from the dust of the ground

Genesis 2:7 (NIV)

Without witnesses, who would believe we were made from dust? Again, some truths are not self-evident.

The experience of computer programming and the knowledge that every pixel on the computer screen, every function, must be coded, helps us to appreciate that each minute cell of the human body had to be created. The complex human eye, heart, and ear did not spontaneously spring into being and coalesce into Man. Just as the whole complex, organized computer did not just manifest in one big bang, so too we must appreciate that two amebae did not wake up one morning and agree to metamorphose into orderly, compatible male and female of a new species. No amount of natural selection could accomplish the parallel development of two compatible, reproducible male and female organisms in tandem. The suggestion that it occurred over millennia is also inconsistent with the immediate need to reproduce in order to survive the biology. Our intelligence may not be receptive to the idea that there is anything greater than we are. However, that conceit does not dispel the real conflicts that the reality has with the science of evolution.

Beliefs from the Bible

Our ancestors have handed down information to us in the story of Adam and Eve that dispenses with these concerns in the Book of Genesis.

Continuing the analogy with computers, evidence of modular programming, a technique that enables a developer to reuse parts of code in other programs (so that, for example, the COPY function and its CONTROL C short cut can be reused in many different applications), provides a vital perspective for us to appreciate similarities in different living organisms. Characteristics of the genome can be explained, not by theories of evolution, but by the truth of a common creator who has all the "modules" of human life at his disposal. The wisdom we gain from the Old Testament is that:

> ... [God] took one of the man's ribs ... Then the Lord God made a woman from the rib he had taken out of the man,
>
> Genesis 2:21-22 (NIV)

The creator of a species has the option to improve on his creation. Genesis tells us that God first created animal life, then created a superior, ruling man:

> God made the wild animals according to their kinds, the livestock according to their kinds, and all the creatures that move along the ground according to their kinds. And God saw that it was good.

> *Then God said, "Let us make mankind in our image, in our likeness, so that they may rule over the fish in the sea and the birds in the sky, over the livestock and all the wild animals, and over all the creatures that move along the ground."*
>
> *Genesis 1:25-26 (NIV)*

In addition to the information on our origins in the Old Testament, there are many places in the New Testament that remind us that we were created in the image and likeness of God and that life is more than the life of our bodies. One such account is the parable of ten maidens with oil lamps in Matthew 25:1-13.

In a nutshell, the story is about ten maidens who each had an oil lamp that they needed to light up their way to a wedding. Five of them had enough oil, and five did not. All ten fell asleep. When they woke, only the five with the extra oil had enough light to allow them to go into the wedding feast.

There is a literal way to read these verses—about lamps and oil. However, a parable is not literal. The lamps are a metaphor that Christ used to bring us the message about our lives. If we revisit the narrative, we will see that the first few words are, *"The kingdom of heaven is like."* This means that the story was used to illustrate something about heaven. The lamp symbolizes the human body. It is a vessel, a container waiting to be filled. The lamps require oil to bring light. As a container on its own, the lamp doesn't perform at all. That message from

Matthew 25 is echoed in John 6, which asserts that the flesh is useless:

> *The Spirit gives life; the flesh counts for nothing. The words I have spoken to you—they are full of the Spirit and life.*
>
> *John 6:63 (NIV)*

In the parable, the maidens symbolize us, people of the flesh. Their lamps filled with oil are our lives of joy and pain, flesh filled with spirit. All the maidens embraced the use of the light from their lamps. That is like our lives. We all experience similar bodily life whether we are Christian, Jewish, agnostic, political, black, white, or whatever. We, like these ten maidens who all had similar oil lamps, have control over our lives just as those maidens decided how much oil to put in their lamps. We make choices. What separates the wise from the foolish maidens in the parable is not the lamp, but the choices about the oil in it. In the parable, five of those maidens were foolish. They did not understand or did not care about the oil in their lamps. In the beginning of the parable they were all waiting for the bridegroom: the host of a grand occasion. The five who knew that they were waiting not only enjoyed the light from their lamps, but had enough oil to wait through until the expected occasion.

The lamps were useless without oil, just as our bodies are of no value without Spirit. What is inside us needs to be filled. The parable is a story behind the truth that the Spirit *inside us* brings light and life. The maidens who enjoyed their lamps only while awake had not prepared for the grand occasion. We must prepare for the time when the body goes to sleep.

In the parable, the 'wise' maidens who had enough oil in their lamps refused to give the others oil when the time came. There is going to be a time for us when it is too late to strengthen our Spirits. The time to gain 'oil' (the wisdom and strength needed for our light to shine eternally) is before sleep comes. Right now, we have opportunities to fill our Spirits. The wise maidens may share their light now, but cannot help after falling asleep. The analogy with lamps fuses the human biology and the human spirit.

Recently, I was unable to access one of my business accounts using a particular computer. Twice previously, pop-up boxes displayed warnings on my screen indicating that I needed to upgrade my operating system. However, I was still allowed to access my account, and I ignored the warnings. Then came the day that I tried to get in but couldn't. I had been comfortable with the old system and it had been inconvenient to upgrade. The warnings had also seemed irrelevant, since I was nevertheless allowed access to my business account.

Sometimes our lives are comfortable and it is inconvenient to do more than is necessary to meet current challenges. It is easy to draw parallels between this and the perspectives of the foolish maidens in the parable. Faced with immediate needs, we may ignore warnings about what is to come.

In Revelation 22, we find many images of prosperity: fruit, a tree of life, a lamb, a river. We are told that there is no darkness there, but that there is light even without lamp or sun: light emanating from God. That analogy takes concepts of light that we know and attempts to provide us a vision of things to come.

In developing a biblical perspective, we do understand the concepts of seeds falling on a dry path and of what is likely to happen to such a seed. We can relate to the idea of seed falling on shallow soil that covers a solid rock surface. Some of us may actually have seen such a plant sprouting out from a light smattering of soil and may also have seen it dry up and wilt in the scorching sun as described in the parable. Even if we have not seen a plant dry up, this is an image that our experience on earth enables us to imagine. Gardeners in our time still pull weeds from among the good plants in the garden, understanding that weeds could get out of control and overcome the good plants. These are all images of this visible, physical world, telling us about the soil, the foundation of our own lives that we do not see: The invisible part of us that is privileged with life eternal. The enhanced perspective is that our mortal life is connected with a higher level of existence.

In the 1950s, if anyone had had a vision of the internet and had tried to describe it, they may have tried various concepts and metaphors. Indeed, in its beginning the internet was popularly described as 'the information superhighway', drawing analogies between traffic on a major highway (already familiar at that time) and the new concepts of data transmission. Expressions such as data traffic entered data processing as people conceived ideas related to concepts that were already familiar.

Jesus spoke of a continuum of life that extends from watchfulness, through to sleep and reawakening, in Matthew 25:1-13, in the parable referred to above in which both wise and foolish "become drowsy" and "fall asleep." This teaching acknowledges that everyone falls asleep, but teaches that some have enough "oil" for the light of reawakening. The Bible also tells us that Jesus lived, died for three days, and came to life again. These examples teach about life's dimensions.

Life after death is a curiosity, and no doubt many of us would like to know of it firsthand. The truth is, we don't know firsthand. Even the tiny minority who claim to have returned can hardly express all there is to know. This reminds me of my first visit to a beautiful Caribbean island that I had read and learned about in school and from visitors who described the beauty of the landscapes, the warmth of the people, the variety of sumptuous foods, the water, sand and every possible thing about the island. Yet, as I touched down at the airport the first time, I was completely unprepared for the accents of the people who spoke to me as I arrived.

The point is, only some dimensions of life are discussed. A discussion of various parts of life is necessarily somewhat disembodied, separating the different dimensions relevant to each particular discussion. We may explain the science of life and how our organs work, recognize that we communicate using an extensive vocabulary of words and a significantly smaller repertory of body language and gestures, acknowledge that we get better at things that are repeated and so learn to creep, to walk, to swim, to drive, to write, by repeated efforts over and over again. Yet, we can hardly explain exactly why, except to say that we are made that way. Scientists can identify our growth hormones and DNA and can explain how things work, how one process has a logical connection to the next and so forth, but cannot explain why, except to say that that is how we are made. Simple questions are answered in terms of *how* it occurs, *how* it is useful, and what happens if things are not that way. Doctors explain what happens if our intestines or our arteries get clogged, and how perfectly the liver and kidney are designed to do what they do, and we sometimes interpret that as why. Yet, *why* is elusive.

Isaiah 5:1-7 explains this in a parallel with grapes grown for a future harvest of wine. That Old Testament vision related by the prophet Isaiah to people in wine country uses a metaphor of a vineyard. Isaiah used images of a winepress, good grapes, wild grapes, a wine tower; the people likely knew personally what the effort to grow grapes involved and understood the profound disappointment of a failed grape crop.

A wine expert in recent times made this statement: "You can make bad wine using good grapes, but never could you make good wine using bad grapes." So, bad grapes meant a useless crop, a complete waste of a whole growing season. It represented a failure of harvest. If you're a farmer and you've worked all year on your crop, it's devastating to find at the end of the harvest that you have nothing.

In essence, the metaphor of bad grapes is a vision of total and utter disappointment in the failures of God's people whose hearts have grown away from Him… a harvest of "wild grapes." As Isaiah tells it:

> … *the vineyard of the Lord of hosts is the house of Israel, And the men of Judah are His pleasant plant. He*

looked for justice, but behold, oppression; For righteousness, but behold, a cry for help.

Isaiah 5:7 (NKJV)

One of the hurdles that skeptics of Christianity encounter is the concept of life powered by the Spirit. Like grapes grown for a future harvest, our lives face an ultimate transformation. Skeptics and believers alike may bloom, but in the final transformation into "wine," it is the output that will reveal the quality of the "grapes." It is not that the grapes don't grow. The cry for help is to put flavor into the grape. So too, the spirit that our body masks requires the flavor of understanding.

In an interesting news item recently, a criminal, before committing a fatal atrocity, smashed his cell phone in an attempt to cover his despicable tracks. Authorities, however, were able to recover telltale information from the apps on his cell phone. One may draw parallels between the relationship between the cell phone and its apps and the relationship between the body and the spirit. Even after the body gets completely smashed, God can recover the Spirit. The Bible also teaches that, no matter the outer being, it is the spirit that gives life (John 6:63). We may take this to mean that despite whatever may be the outer poses, it is the spirit that *gives* life.

The legend that the famous Italian painter Leonardo Da Vinci used live models for his painting The Last Supper provides an engaging illustration. The painting depicts Jesus and his twelve disciples at supper together for the last time. Supposedly, the model Da Vinci used to depict the pure, holy image of Jesus was a suave, unblemished nineteen-year-old young man. He also used other models in his effort to depict each of the disciples. Six years later, he found the perfect model to use for Judas, the unsavory character of the twelve. The scarred, battered twenty-five-year-old criminal that Leonardo Da Vinci found in a prison dungeon satisfied the artist's need for a completely hateful model to pose for the villain of the painting. According to legend, Da Vinci unknowingly selected the same model he had used when he painted the holy Jesus six years earlier.

If we use only our eyes, we fail to see the life of a person. In acknowledging the expanded dimensions of our daily lives, we recognize that we are more than flesh and bone. Who we are is encased in that body, that flesh. Who we are learns and gains knowledge and strength, and is ultimately freed of physical confines when the body dies.

Without witnesses, who would believe? Some truths are not self-evident. One can indeed observe increasing levels of sophistication if organisms are arrayed from amoeba to man. So too can one observe increasing levels of sophistication if we compare the Ford Model T with the 2016 Ford RS. Perhaps one model did advance from the other, and no doubt we can tabulate the items of progressive distinction. It did not happen automatically. The questions are, how come? Who did it? Evolution and natural selection are compelling hypotheses that many people believe.

Belief in the Theory of Evolution

The theory of evolution was originally presented by Charles Darwin. The premise is that man has evolved from lower animals. A very interesting theory! Yet it fails to explain why the lower animals still exist after they have evolved; why the "missing link" has nevertheless disappeared, despite its constitution supposedly superior to its earlier links and the principle of natural selection in the evolutionary chain. If natural selection preserves the best genes, why has man not continued to evolve? If indeed evolution is progressive, why did we lose our fur/ hair, considering its natural advantage in extreme weather?

The theory also uses similarities between the species to propose evolution as the only possible cause. It overlooks that the same elements used in one creation could be applied and improved in others. It denies any intervention of the creator. Using that tunnel vision, one would be tempted to propose that because of their chronology in technology development, today's cell phones evolved from yesterday's dial up phones with no intervention by their creators. Quite simply, chronological sequence of species is not proof of evolution.

Evolution has been blessed with the shroud of science beginning from the earliest time of its conception. School science classes today revere evolution, and it holds firm on curricula in the United States, in preference to other beliefs such as the belief that God is real and that there is more to humanity than the evidence of the biological presence. Schools in the US stopped teaching these beliefs around 1970 and the belief that evolution is truth usurped its position on school curricula. Today, educated believers in God are often ashamed or reticent about truths of creation in deference to their respect for science. But how did the evolutionary belief find its way into the realm of science?

Science is founded on proof and may be inspired by theory. The theory of evolution first proposed by Charles Darwin has never been proven. As a belief, it is extremely intriguing and persuasive. As a scientific conclusion, it has many flaws when examined on principles that must be upheld if a theory is to be regarded as science. Evolution is a belief.

Mistaking similarity for dependency, proponents of evolutionary theory use scientific evidence of progressively complex life forms and of stages of life as proof of dependence of one form of life on another and of automatic progression of individual organisms from one stage of life to another. To evolutionists, increasing complexity means that one form evolved into the other without any intervention, without the action we call creation. For example, evolutionists regard changes in fossil evidence over time as demonstration of systemic propulsion they call evolution.

Evolutionists peddle the ability of creatures to evolve in response to environmental needs. Touting evidence of similarity between land and water creatures, we are given the understanding that fish evolved gills to breathe in water, and that because the cell structure of some fish fossils is similar to those of human lungs, we share a common ancestor. Creationists say we share a common creator. There are gaps in the reasoning that an ancient fish somehow survived long enough to ditch its gills, find a mate, reproduce and spawn the human race. Similarities in DNA of ancient fossil fish do not cross those hurdles without a creator.

Observing similarities between human and aquatic cells, scientists conclude that humans carry evidence of an aquatic past in our bodies, yet fail to explain how we travelled that evolutionary road into today's man. If this were consistent with reality, why fear our ability to transform in response to new realities such as global warming?   If such transformation were scientific truth, we could expect that survivors would be a superior New Man. Scientists' actions show that they know that that is not so. We address issues like global warming because we know that it is the way people deal with environmental change and man does not transform into new species.

Science is our friend. The strict scientific process produces authentic results. Conclusions with regard to the evidence of evolution, however, need further review. They do not adhere to the strict demands of science. Conclusions clash with the hard evidence of the human condition. The missing link, it seems, is not biological; it is conceptual.

One part of the misconception is the belief that one primate, based on genetic selection and some environmental change, evolved into man. Savant children and talented ancestors throughout human history (Thomas Edison and Nikola Tesla in the sciences; Tchaikovsky and Chopin; Leonardo Da Vinci and Michelangelo; Madame Curie and Amelia Earhart, and the like) have not been precursors to a new breed. Indeed, their direct descendants have not even led to a superior family line or similar fame, much less a new race, and none to a new species. So, where are you, superior gene, in this process of genetic selection? If a single primate could indeed have spawned this new human gene, then the whole idea of heredity as a factor in the life of a gene is flawed. An interesting theory, a respected belief, but the belief in evolution is contradicted by hard empirical evidence of the human condition.

Mating with another human is one way that the stability of the genetic framework of humanity is preserved. It is the reason that a simple examination of the children of talented humans demonstrates no tendency toward genius and may in cases show the opposite. Two parents are required, not one. Even without a search for fossil evidence, human life is rife with these examples. The offspring of athletes do not routinely show any special talent in the athletic arena. For the hypothesis of natural selection to be sound, one should be able to predict and demonstrate that when there is some evidence of superiority in the human species, the offspring shows the same superiority. This is clearly not the case. It is therefore not science to say that man's superiority evolved from another species based on genetic selection. It is a belief that supports the theory of evolution, but neither of the two is scientific in the true sense of the word. They fail as science, both in their logical conceptualization and on the stage of proof.

Given that reproduction in man requires two participants, the belief in evolution also falters as a scientific proposal in its failure to explain how the one supposedly superior genetic specimen evolved simultaneously with its reproductive partner, compatible in every detail. It is an interesting theory, but again, evaluated against scientific logic and empirical evidence, it is lacking. Creationists propose that God created a mate using genetic material from the original creation.

According to Sir Isaac Newton, science must necessarily show "observable, empirical and measurable evidence, subject to specific principles of reasoning." Science has not found such evidence of evolution. The idea of a biological missing link is ill-conceived. Given the presumed superiority, we would not have needed to search. How could it succumb in a way that neither its (weaker) predecessors nor its supposed successor (man) did? Why the search? Indeed, he should be right there, grandfathering Man into the future.

The theory of evolution also ignores the reality that human life is greater than its biology and ignores the evidence of the human spirit. Enlightened perspectives recognize that human life includes dimensions of life beyond biology, and direct us to the source of a fulfilled life. Evolution overlooks that this fulfillment is participatory, not systemic.

In 2009, National Geographic published a well-received article, reporting that the missing link was found in Germany, a 47-million-year-old fossil that they named Ida. They created a big media splash that was expected to make waves among those who study human origins.[1] The term "missing link" refers to the gap between theory and reality. A theory is accepted as reality by the scientific community if that missing link completes the logic of and evidences the reasoning in the theory.

Describing Ida, a 2011 National Geographic article explained:

> *About 40 million years ago, there were two distinct primate groups: prosimians and anthropoids. One way taxonomists separate prosimians and anthropoids is by their noses. Prosimians, or strepsirrhini, have dog-like, wet noses. Extant, or living, representatives of strepsirrhini include lemurs, lorises, and bush babies. Anthropoids, or haplorhini, have dry noses. Extant representatives of haplorhini include monkeys and apes. Humans are also dry-nosed primates. At some point during the Eocene, primates evolved into these two different branches.[2]*

Over the years, scientists have unearthed many fossils in pursuit of searches for "the missing link." Trustworthy scientific findings help us understand different life forms and establish better understanding of their chronology using respected scientific techniques. Trusting the scientific process,

---

[1] http://news.nationalgeographic.com/news/2009/05/090519-missing-link-found.html

[2] http://www.nationalgeographic.org/news/who-was-ida/

one can accept that findings depict some chronology. Technical errors and hoaxes in some reports do not disprove all other scientific findings. Ultimately, the checks and balances in the scientific process can be expected to resolve problems encountered along the way. The premise that the chronology is synonymous with evolution is one of those problems. It is illogical, unscientific, a *non-sequitur* because there are other explanations. One does not have to be a scientist to prove that things occurring simultaneously or consecutively, or things made of similar material, do not necessarily emerge from each other or are in any way dependent on each other. Neither genetic composition of a fossil nor its chronology prove claims of descendancy.

The ethics of science demands that scientists admit that the gap between primates and man reflects intervention rather than systemic propulsion. Where did the specimen get its new gene? Whatever scientists choose to label that intervention, if the understanding of human history is to uphold respected Newtonian scientific principles, it must be recognized that a biological gap is not consistent with the biological makeup of humans. Had it existed, such a superior biological specimen must have thrived; its supposed predecessors have.

In summary, that gap, that intervening presence, is what Christians know as God. The process that produced a human being superior in every way to the predecessor species is creation. Science identifies genetic similarities in the various species that Christians attribute to a single creator. Similar to the way Microsoft products reflect similarity in their constituency and interface despite the different roles in Excel, Word, and Visual Studio within the Windows world, so too do animals and humans, despite similarities in their constituency, occupy different places in this world, reflecting the imprint of their single creator. Analyzing and sequencing genes gives us a better understanding of the composition of our bodies. It is consistent with creationism and discredits assumptions of evolution.

No one can argue with the belief in evolution. It is, however, misleading for the field of science -- built on stringent principles, supported by a history of consistent proof -- to promote the belief in evolution as science.

Reflect and Explore:

A) What do you understand about the lamp metaphor in Matthew 25:1-13?

B) What are your views about the analysis of hardware, software and life?

C) Can you see any benefit in using metaphors rather than speaking plainly?

D) How would you explain what life is if someone (child or adult) asked you?

E) What theories about life were you taught in school or elsewhere that differ from the perspectives shared in this chapter?

Chapter 3: Life Well Lived

We each are body, mind and spirit. As we explored different concepts of life in the last chapter, we acknowledged evidence that humans are more than physical beings. Your body is the physique or physical manifestation of YOU. The spirit is the psyche, akin to the psychological presence of the human person. Indeed, it is the spirit that is the seat of the person. While the body *manifests* you, the spirit *is* you: the defining essence of person, character, and temperament that makes one person happy in the rain and another miserable, though equally wet. On a third plane, our minds are the sponges of learning and experience that enable us to be dynamic beings and help us develop understanding. Human beings can process new thoughts and ideas, learn new skills and languages and add new perceptions and concepts. We create new theories -- even new words and languages -- we create and improve on tools and technologies, buildings and structures in the same way that we create and improve on perception, ideas and knowledge. Lives well lived include all the planes and dimensions we perceive -- physical, spiritual and mental. Other planes that we tend to overlook include dreams and sleep. Possibly, planes and dimensions we do not yet perceive are also part of our lives.

Many have had their say concerning the path to a well lived life. Some pursue all their opportunities on the physical plane. Those sculpt and shape their bodies and seek ever challenging adventures, stimulating their bodies in increasing levels, seeking, climbing, flying, sky diving... all on one plane.

In recent times, we have had Steven Covey and his perceptions of the Ten Habits of Highly Effective People, Dr. Rick Warren and his prescriptions for a Purpose Driven Life, and other celebrated writers and inspirational leaders pointing us to various paths leading to a good life. Each writer holds only a shard of the complex puzzle of life.

Each of us is different; we have in common the bases of *being* but differ in the realities of each individual human being. Analysis of *being* and what it means to *be* is an ongoing pursuit. With that caveat, I define it as the collaboration of human body, mind and spirit. That is human being. Life copiously, abundantly lived is the epitome of intellect, spirituality and physicality. A life well lived embodies accomplishments that include mental, spiritual and physical realization. Many of us are fortunate to embrace a good life with some level of comfort in one of those areas. The best of us accomplish some level of competence in more than one of those planes. Popular culture today encourages us to function as mediocre people and recognize each other for excellence in <u>one</u> plane, even if we sink to the depths of despair in others. Celebrated artists and great leaders alike are flawed in particular ways but are celebrated in popular culture. An excellent voice, a beautiful face, an unfailing stroke, a golden touch: they all get us a free pass into social prominence, to stand up as an example for others to follow. It is a cultural norm to function only on one human plane of existence.

As people, we admire, compliment and reward individuals who succeed in something. Often, we overlook that life is multidimensional and can be nurtured and developed on different planes. A life well lived is not lived on one plane alone, but is experienced supremely in plentiful dimensions on each plane of existence.

Plentiful Dimensions

To thoroughly address this statement, we can examine the planes and dimensions. I have broadly defined the planes as physical, spiritual and mental. Many human dimensions can be grouped within them. These include skills, talents, abilities, activities and deliberate work and effort as well as arts, crafts, technical, scientific, culinary, medical, and a long list of learned abilities that are developed with instruction and practice. On the other hand, there are human dimensions such as sight and speech that are considered 'natural'.

In other words, human life is governed by the physical, mental and spiritual strengths but it extends beyond natal, biological or genetic gifts. Social interaction, communications and the benefits of teaching and learning experiences are expert facilitators of human life, constantly shaping, informing, and structuring a perfect fitting. Also, some dimensions are interdependent and not completely contained within a single plane.

Physical Life

One does not have to deny the body to believe in God and the Spirit. Our human presence is equally real. Life is confirmed by our physical existence, promoted by the health of our bodies and enhanced by cultural approaches to grooming, appropriate dress, behavior and more. Life lived abundantly on the physical plane is as active as a person's genetics and health permit. It maintains and stretches itself from the wealth of knowledge about the physical body. It therefore takes cues from the mental sphere. Along with the biological characteristics of the body, inputs to abundant physical life include the sciences of exercise, diet, water, rest, health care and related knowledge. Cultivating and following through on healthy behaviors, habits and activities intelligently is the key to abundant physical life.

Science and research sometimes change this intelligence. For example, at one time it is good to eat eggs, while at another that is deemed unhealthy; one arm of research finds fault with coffee and another cites benefits; the pill we take today may be found tomorrow to do harm to our bodies. The truth is that whatever we do, our bodies will eventually succumb to something. Abundant physical life is the ability to do our best with the health we have while we live. If we ignore the demands of physical health, our lives today will be compromised and we will likely be unable to embrace the healthy abundance open to us.

With healthful physical lives, we are able to follow through on our talents and gifts, perform the simple activities required of our daily lives, learn and do more. Gifts of the Spirit are aided and supported by healthy bodies. In his message to the Galatians (Galatians 5:22) the Apostle Paul explained how powerful the direction of the Spirit is in our lives. The Spirit guides us to show love, joy, peace, patience, kindness, goodness, gentleness, to be true, and to keep the body under control. So, when Paul said:

> *But if you are led by the Spirit, you are not under the law.*
>
> *Galatians 5:18 (NIV)*

Paul was not telling the Galatians that they should break the law and consider themselves above it. Instead, he was telling them that the gifts of the Spirit lead us to do good and there is no law against doing good.

We can embrace the abundant joys of living, loving and sharing our lives and talents beyond merely maintaining daily life. Some human needs are not fulfilled by physical living alone. We observe, in the most extreme, people in a vegetative state—physically alive, but unable to fulfill the promise of life. It is human to learn. Living life only on the physical plane may lead to the misery of unfulfilled needs, aimlessness and the depths of despair (even when there is physical success) as the body fails to satisfy the other dimensions that support whole life.

The Exponential Human Mind

There is a relationship between our physical and mental experiences. Our mental lives are fed by education which, in one dimension, is dependent on observation, hearing and reading and often reflected in our written, behavioral and spoken communications. The other dimension -- formal education -- includes controlled experiments, teaching syllabi and required readings. In contrast, informally we learn what we see and hear in our families, communities, media and from our peers. Living life abundantly as educated people involves grasping the wealth of knowledge that can be gathered from these sources and selectively and appropriately applying it in our lives. Abundant living is therefore not merely acquiring a certificate or being awarded a highly respected qualification, but *living* abundantly with and by the abundance of knowledge and information accessible by our minds. Certificates may hang impressively on walls or be displayed with pride in albums, but lives lived with mental abundance throb with the relevant application of state-of-the-art knowledge and information and shine in the dark dimensions of community and world needs, giving abundantly from life's bounty.

In that way, mental life and abundance are interrelated with the physical. By extension, it is influenced by and can be determined by how we care for our physical bodies and all the wholesome or destructive ways of life that affect physical well-being. Given these interrelationships, social environment and genetics can equally exert influence on abundant mental life. On the one hand, the encouragement and persuasion to pursue one learning activity or another is an element of socialization, while on the other, its roots are not immune to the influence of genetics. One's mind plays a role in living life abundantly, and one's physical conditions are not only themselves a dimension of abundant life, but also have an impact on one's mental wealth.

The fact that our mental lives are fed by both education and physical capacity often hides the influence of social circumstance. Social circumstance, including family, culture and neighborhood as well as politics, economics, beliefs and the like can restrict or facilitate access to basic tools such as reading and writing on which education is fed. You don't have to be highly educated to live an abundant mental life. However, the pursuit of other dimensions of abundant life may require you to navigate particular social systems. When we don't ourselves possess the access needed to the basic tools, we must align with those who do, or acquire them ourselves. I have seen parents unable to read receive required support from their children. Various social institutions also provide needed support to help navigate the paths of abundant living, whether academic, informational, professional, hobby or other guidance or support is needed.

There is general consensus about mental and physical life and we test each other in competition to stretch and grow in these dimensions. It is no wonder humans attain and increase levels of physical and intellectual accomplishment.

Spirited Life

For approximately six years, I watched as a family member suffered increasing levels of physical incapacity.

Combined with increasing decline in the ability to communicate, it seemed that both physical and mental capacity declined, but it was never determined just how agile the mind was, except in relation to the strength or weakness of particular physical abilities. Throughout this period however, it was clear that her Spirit remained intact. There was no way to measure the Spiritual presence, but we each could individually attest to the calm, alert presence of that Spirit. As I spent time with her daily over that six years, I became acutely aware of the distinction between the Spirit and the mind and body. Although they need each other in order to connect and communicate with this world, they are separately alive. A strong spirit thrives despite the ravages of physical or mental incapacity. Reference was made earlier to slaves who triumphed and emerged after the ordeal, whole of spirit and mentally strong. The point is that spiritual life is not debilitated by those things that deny abundant physical life.

The supreme experience of life stems from living an abundant spiritual life. Even the most highly educated person at the epitome of physical health and with an accumulation of material wealth could plod along without rich, abundant experiences. I am not referring to rich possessions, but to happy life bubbling over with joy and saturated with peace. A strong healthful spirit is needed to fulfill the abundant potential of mind and body. Happiness and goodwill come from the spirit. Generosity and kindness may be easily accomplished through possessions, but are inspired by the spirit. Giving, a physical act, is stirred by the bounty of spirit. The yearning to give because there is need springs from spiritual wealth; wanting to give because you have plenty is different because it is reasoned from the store of one's wealth. Generosity in all forms nurtures abundant life and may tap in to physical wealth and possessions in some manner, but spiritual abundance is a function of grace. It does not spring from wealthy possessions, though it is generally manifested in tangible giving. This helps us understand Christ's statements to a rich man on how to inherit the promised blessing of life. He later told his disciples:

> ...it is easier for a camel to go through the eye of a needle than for a rich man to enter the kingdom of God.
> Matthew 19:24 (NKJV)

The difficulty is that giving from wealth takes into consideration how much is given and involves measured concerns of preserving the wealth. That is practical and makes sense. Hard earned wealth (and even easy gotten wealth) helps us to enhance our physical lives and status and to provide a source for our giving. The colloquial saying, "a fool and his money will soon be parted" speaks to the social wisdom of our time. The dilemma of the rich man is that spiritual giving may seem to be social folly.

Spiritual abundance is also reflected in showing mercy, sharing knowledge, encouraging others, attending to the needs of others, teaching about any of the dimensions of life and showing others how to live. Ultimately, spiritual abundance is also cultivated by these strengths. Some of these require or are enhanced by learning. Doing more for others, for example, may require learning the subject matter or developing the skill. Other strengths may need the support of good health. In other words, <u>living</u> a spiritually abundant life is not merely conceptual, but is interrelated with our healthful minds and bodies. However, wherever we are physically and mentally, there is room for spiritual abundance.

Every year, some Christians observe a period of physical denial, called Lent, before celebrating the death and resurrection of Jesus Christ. The period is observed by various church groups in different ways. However, its usefulness is as an opportunity for people to train and practice asserting the Spirit over the demands of the body. The foods and fun given up are the physical aspect, while the practice of submission of behaviors to the Spirit is the opportunity to practice behaving on other terms.

While spiritual gifts reflect or manifest in generous, abundant actions, spiritual abundance is a spring inside. Romans 12:6-8 identifies seven gifts of the spirit that we will examine later in this book: prophecy, ministry, teaching, encouragement, giving, leading, and mercy. Using these gifts requires one to tap into the core of the human spirit, fueling abundant living.

Spiritual abundance is alive. It is the power that fuels our bodies and inspires our minds. You can't see it, even if you dissect the body. It is seen in joy, service, kindness, laughter, giving, sharing and wholesome living. The phrase I embrace for describing spiritual abundance is found in Ephesians 1:18: "the eyes of your heart." Living with spiritual abundance demands that we see through "the eyes of our hearts:" that we reach beyond the physical dimensions and embrace life with kindness and hope.

As much as spiritual abundance is *manifested* in these ways and seen in these acts, it comes from God and His grace. We can be guided by others, but no person can make us spiritually aware. According to Ephesians 3:6-12, this grace is open to everyone. There is no need to join up or sign up or pay up to receive it. A simple request to God in faith for strength and power through his Spirit opens one's inner being to this grace. It is granted at God's will. While we can work at physical and mental abundance, spiritual abundance requires that we have faith and trust not our will, but God's.

Those who do not believe may find the explanation above frustratingly inadequate. If spiritual abundance and finding God both require faith, if you don't have faith, you can't find either of them. I imagine that that is extremely frustrating for those who want to engage in a real search for God, or someone whose faith is shaken. I understand that and have searched for a truth that I can share with someone who does not believe in God or the Bible. What I can say is that if you have pursued the epitome of physical living, explored your mental capacities and are still unfulfilled after you have exercised and eaten well, avoided abusive drugs and behaviors and followed through on what you have learned about staying well; if you have pursued a hobby, skill or talent that utilizes your physical gifts and followed through on the learning that could help you to refine and enjoy your talents and the gifts of your mind and are still unfulfilled -- then you are primed to discover another dimension of yourself. More simply, the journey may be started by reading the scriptures. Finding Christian friends is also helpful. As you search, the churches that welcome you as you are may be a source of spiritual enlightenment. You may also find the prayer following this chapter helpful.

The Bible encourages both physical and spiritual training:

physical training is of some value, but godliness has value for all things, holding promise for both the present life and the life to come.

1 Timothy 4:8 (NIV)

Spirit and spiritual life, unlike physical life and mental acuity, are not concrete, touchable realities. Spiritual strength manifests itself in peace. You can read whole libraries about exercise and diet, water, sunscreen, sleep and hygiene. One can pursue PhD studies, challenge the brain with a plethora of Sudoku and other puzzles, memory competitions and more intellectual learning opportunities than one can pursue in a single lifetime. Yet, to develop spiritual strength is to be at peace. The question is how to do it.

In our quest to conquer the challenges of our physical world, modern cultures have developed extensive vocabulary to describe and overcome the heights of mountains and rummage the depths of oceans; the intricacies of DNA and the magnitude of tsunamis, but hardly any word beyond "peace" is used to describe the harmony of self and the truths of the human spirit.

Peace is known, therefore, more by the absence of disturbance and active violence than by an analysis of its inner components. I can only assert that there is spiritual life, and propose that after an individual has conquered the mountains of physical journey and explored the avenues of mind, it may become easier to recognize that there is an unexplored facet to abundant living.

Someone willing to follow through with the eyes of the heart has to overcome their accustomed reliance on eyes, ear, tongue, touch and smell. The eyes of the heart reach beyond those. To see with the heart may be a process of learning, a journey that may be cultivated by habit instead of a particular act or event. In practice, such a quest may be affected by habits, relationships and commitments, including jobs and responsibilities. There is no formula that would meet diverse needs. Instead, one must find some time to pursue the process. The Bible recommends one day weekly to devote to Spiritual needs. That may be a start, and visiting a church may open suitable opportunities to learn.

I trust that, as the apostle Paul prayed for the Ephesians, that "the eyes of your heart may be enlightened in order that you may know the hope to which he has called you, the riches of his glorious inheritance in his holy people." (Ephesians 1:18, NIV)

Reflect and Explore:

> A) What are your views about the dimensions of life presented in this chapter?

B) Thinking of your own skills, chores and hobbies, do you see different dimensions?

C) Discuss resources that are available in your neighborhood to help people live abundantly. Make a list of these resources and share the list. Are they consistent with dimensions of abundant living discussed in this chapter?

D) Read Ephesians 3.

E) PERSONAL ASSIGNMENT #1: Take some time to reflect on your own life, how you feel and any help and resources that you may need.

F) PERSONAL ASSIGNMENT #2: Devote increasingly more time each week to the needs you identify in the personal assignment.

Prayer for Spiritual Strength

based on

Ephesians 3:14-21

For this reason I kneel before the Father, from whom every family in heaven and on earth derives its name. I pray that out of his glorious riches he may strengthen me with power through his Spirit in my inner being, so that Christ may dwell in my heart through faith. And I pray that I, being rooted and established in love, may have power, together with all the Lord's holy people, to grasp how wide and long and high and deep is the love of Christ, and to know this love that surpasses knowledge—that I may be filled to the measure of all the fullness of God.

Now to him who is able to do immeasurably more than all we ask or imagine, according to his power that is at work within us, to him be glory in the church and in Christ Jesus throughout all generations, for ever and ever! Amen.

Chapter 4: The Kingdom of Heaven

The term "heaven" refers to the abode of God and the destination of good souls. The Bible also refers to God's "kingdom," which conveys to us the concept of rulership by and of some sovereign constituent. Indeed, the Bible often refers to heaven in juxtaposition with earth, developing the perspective not only that heaven is different from earth, but also that heaven and earth together sum up the sphere of life.

Other references to the heavens in the Bible are tangible elements like rain, clouds, frost, fire, moon, and the like. We are also told that:

> "...The heavens will disappear with a roar; the elements will be destroyed by fire, and the earth and everything done in it will be laid bare." (2 Peter 3:10, NIV)

In contrast, heaven, the abode of God, is attainable after life on earth as we know it ceases: that is, after we die. Heaven is exalted above the heavens (Ephesians 4:10) and its 'elements' are intangible. God speaks and "thunders" (2 Samuel 22:14) from heaven, and is not contained by heaven (1 Kings 8:27). The Book of Deuteronomy guides us to this perspective of the heavenly array. Specifically:

> "...when you look up to the sky and see the sun, the moon and the stars—all the heavenly array—do not be

enticed into bowing down to them and worshiping things the Lord your God has apportioned to all the nations under heaven." (Deuteronomy 4:19, NIV)

So, going to heaven is not the same as physically living in the clouds. They are different concepts that may cause confusion. We do not know where (physically) heaven is, but the Bible provides guidance through language about what heaven is.

While we do not know where heaven is located, the Bible records that Jesus was "taken up" (Acts 1:9, NIV), and that after the ascension the disciples were "looking intently up" (Acts 1:10, NIV). Solidifying the concept of Heaven being above or out of visual range, is the promise, not only that Jesus will return in the same manner that he left, (Acts 1:11) but also that that return will be visible to all:

For as lightning that comes from the east is visible even in the west, so will be the coming of the Son of Man.
Matthew 24:27 (NIV)

Although as perceived by the eye, heaven may appear to be "up," other senses may perceive heaven as a sense of joy, growth (as in seeds); transformation (like yeast); awe inspiring (as in precious pearls); and more. Different expressions such as "going to heaven," as well as figurative language are used in the Bible to refer to the Kingdom of life after death.

Jesus described heaven as a kingdom with treasure hidden in a field, so precious that when a man found it, he gave up everything he owned to buy that field. These descriptions are mostly found in parables and analogies, metaphors and similes that give us clues. These (some below), together explain the experience of life after death:

Clues to the Kingdom

A) "The kingdom of heaven is like treasure hidden in a field. When a man found it, he hid it again, and then in his joy went and sold all he had and bought that field." (Matt 13:44, NIV)

B) The kingdom of heaven is like a man who sowed good seed in his field. (Matt 13:24, NIV)

C) "This is what the kingdom of God is like. A man scatters seed on the ground. Night and day, whether he sleeps or gets up, the seed sprouts and grows, though he does not know how. All by itself the soil produces grain." (Mark 4:26-28, NIV)

D) "The kingdom of heaven is like a mustard seed, which a man took and planted in his field." (Matt 13:31, NIV)

E) "At that time, the kingdom of heaven will be like ten virgins who took their lamps and went out to meet the bridegroom." (Matt 25:1, NIV)

But what does this all mean? The images conjured by each of these references are so diverse that there is no single likeness to be recognized. Seeds, a bridegroom, oil lamps! Apparently, the experience of heaven, rather than being like each single metaphor or simile, is quite distinct from any one of the experiences we have had and are having on earth. Instead, different dimensions of the experience may be compared with, or are similar to, but are not exactly the same as (hence the "like" similes) particular experiences we know on earth. Comparisons also abound from many activities familiar to us:

F) "The kingdom of heaven is like yeast that a woman took and mixed into about sixty pounds of flour until it worked all through the dough." (Matt 13:33, NIV)

G) "Again, the kingdom of heaven is like a merchant looking for fine pearls. When he found one of great value, he went away and sold everything he had and bought it." (Matt 13:45-46, NIV)

H) "Once again, the kingdom of heaven is like a net that was let down into the lake and caught all kinds of fish." (Matt 13:47, NIV)

I) "The kingdom of heaven is like a king who prepared a wedding banquet for his son." (Matt 22:2, NIV)

J) "Therefore, the kingdom of heaven is like a king who wanted to settle accounts with his servants." (Matt 18:23, NIV)

K) "Again, it will be like a man going on a journey, who called his servants and entrusted his wealth to them." (Matt 25:14, NIV)

L) "The kingdom of heaven is like a landowner who went out early in the morning to hire workers for his vineyard." (Matt 20:1, NIV)

As I expressed in the first chapter, the dominion of heaven is as unlike our world as our world is to the unborn baby in a womb; the unborn chick in an eggshell; the sedentary caterpillar riveted to a branch. The effort to explain the foreign concept of the kingdom of heaven uses not only concrete images of seeds and pearls, baking and pearl fishing, but also more abstract and hazy concepts:

M) "...the kingdom of God is in your midst." (Luke 17:21, NIV)

N) "...he will separate the people one from another as a shepherd separates the sheep from the goats." (Matt 25:32, NIV)

O) "Where there is a dead body, there the vultures will gather." (Luke 17:37, NIV)

P) "The kingdom of God is not a matter of eating and drinking, but of righteousness, peace and joy in the Holy Spirit." (Romans 14:17, NIV)

Q) "But Christ has indeed been raised from the dead, the firstfruits of those who have fallen asleep." (1 Cor. 15:20, NIV)

R) "...The one who is victorious will not be hurt at all by the second death." (Rev. 2:11, NIV)

My vision from all this is that heaven, though not a physical place, may be thought of in terms of the attributes or properties of some things we know, like a small seed, a precious pearl. In essence, a tiny part of each of us that has the potential to expand the way a mustard seed produces something quite unlike its original self; or the way yeast expands; or the way the value of a single pearl or treasure can encompass everything one owns. This tiny part, perhaps our soul, is greater than the sum total of our bodies, and possesses extensive potential more precious than the lives we know. This suggests to me that the experience after death will be for each of us greater than our experience of this world. Apart from magnitude other implications are evident:

We find the parable of the sower in Matthew 13. This time, Jesus' message to us is the idea that we are all of the same seed, but that it is the soil, the foundations on which we rest our lives, that differentiates between temporary and enduring success. Using ideas we could relate to, Jesus conveyed what he termed "the secrets of the kingdom of heaven" (Matthew 13:11, NIV). The secret is that just as seeds don't grow and endure based on where they are from or what they are, but through the soil that nurtures them, so too we as humans will grow differently and manifest different lives; for some of us that life will endure eternally.

A metaphor Jesus Christ used is the parable of the great wedding banquet. In it, he describes this other life we would experience after our bodies die in terms of a grand feast or banquet. In a nutshell, the parable (Matthew 22:2) tells of a wealthy king who prepares a wedding banquet, but the invited guests fail to show up, even after messengers are sent to call them. Eventually, the king extends the invitation to everyone nearby, who happen to be properly dressed. The message in this parable seems to be the need not just to expect a grand kingdom, but also to ready ourselves so that we can accept the invitation when the time comes. Those originally invited can be overlooked in preference for those who are ready. When the invitation comes, if we aren't ready, we can be thrown out of the "wedding."

The parables in Matthew 22:2 and 18:23 imply that in heaven we will be hosted by a grand, magnanimous ruler (like a king); who is seeking to reward his beloved (son) lavishly (as in a wedding banquet); and justly repay (settle accounts with) those who serve him (servants). These two parables together imply to me that heaven is simultaneously indulgent and equitable.

The parable in Matthew 25:14 suggests that the abundance of heaven is reaped from the wealth of life's nurturing experiences, as the man going on the long journey rewarded abundantly those servants who did most with the wealth he entrusted to them. Yet the parable of the landowner hiring workers for his vineyard (Matt 20:1) simultaneously implies an evenhandedness with respect to time. Taken together these suggest that the fullness of life experience, not length of life, predisposes one to rich after-death experiences. This suggestion of the fullness of life experience is carried on in the parable of the wise and foolish virgins. The spirit so filled with wisdom can thrive after death (which plagues wise and foolish alike) and endure the darkness (sleep) that precedes the new life (marriage to the bridegroom) (Matt 25:1). These implications about the fullness of our lives are continued in the assertion that the kingdom we inherit from God is in our midst (Matt 17:21).

When Jesus spoke with the Pharisees, he used the analogy of dead bodies and vultures gathering. In contrast, when he used a descriptive analogy, he spoke of heaven as a place of peace and joy. We learn that heaven is not a matter of food, drink or pain. In each, Jesus was trying to communicate a 'foreign' concept we call heaven, and how our lives on earth lead us there, using language familiar to each different group of people. It is one truth, with many different dimensions.

In John 10, Christ used the sheep pen as an analogy for salvation. It invokes the image of a safe place watched over by a care-giver, the shepherd. For the agrarian people to whom Christ was speaking, the analogy would have been complete. Christ explained the analogy, pointing out that the gatekeeper opens the gate for the sheep, calls the sheep, and leads them to safety, and those who follow his lead would similarly find safety.

Being unfamiliar myself with the nature of sheep, I investigated and discovered sheep are natural followers, and respond only to the voice of the shepherd, master/ owner. Sheep generally don't follow instructions given by strangers, and they hear when their owner speaks. Understanding this leads us to appreciate Christ's way of telling us, as he spoke with people familiar with the ways of sheep, that through him we find green pastures: more specifically, life and rich nourishment.

Unlike these indirect messages, the message in Romans 14:17 is direct: the kingdom of God is not a matter of eating and drinking, but of righteousness, peace and joy in the Holy Spirit. In a nutshell then the stature of God is greater than heaven, the home of God, and we can look forward to 'good' experiences in the home of God.

The New International Version (NIV) of the Bible has over forty references to sheep. The many references help us understand the link between us, God and heaven. Continuing the link to life after death, the analogy in Matthew 24:22 tells us that God will separate his sheep from other life (goats) on earth. There is no pressure on anyone to believe this. God will recognize his sheep.

Many Mansions

Jesus told his disciples of many mansions in the Kingdom of God. This conveys the image of many different options for residence in God's house. Yet it also appears that Jesus has one place prepared so that his disciples could be with him.

In my Father's house are many mansions: if it were not so, I would have told you. I go to prepare a place for you.

And if I go and prepare a place for you, I will come again, and receive you unto myself; that where I am, there ye may be also.

And whither I go ye know, and the way ye know.

...

I am the way, the truth, and the life: no man cometh unto the Father, but by me.

John 14:2-4 & 6, (KJV)

Although the concept of other mansions is intriguing, I will not explore it in this writing. Suffice it to understand that there is a place prepared for each person who is a disciple of Christ.

Paradise Found

Paradise is another hoped-for prize. In popular usage, the word paradise connotes a sense of bliss, happiness and beauty. It is used three times in the Bible to refer to a destination after death: Firstly, in Luke 23:43, it is the place that Jesus expected to meet the two condemned men crucified with him; then in 2 Cor. 12:4, it is described as a place where "inexpressible things" that "no one is permitted to tell" are heard. A third reference to paradise is found in the Revelation, as a promise for those who are victorious. That reference also presents the tree of life:

> To the one who is victorious, I will give the right to eat from the tree of life, which is in the paradise of God. (Revelation 2:7, NIV)

Different from popular usage, the word paradise, according to www.etymonline.com, was originally from Late Latin *paradises* and from the Greek word *paradeisos,* meaning "garden" or "park." It may originally have been used to refer to the place where souls are tended, cared for and find refuge, as in a garden or park, in contrast to the open wild or wilderness where there is aimless drifting with no sense of direction.

For me, the belief in eternal life is not an egotistical fear of death or need to believe that there is more than this to life. This would be adequate if it were all. Instead, I feel the strength of my spirit and the sense of its independence from my body. I realized that when I was diagnosed with cancer, I too was initially caught up in the hype of the horror of that illness. I say hype not because the horror is not real, but because any potentially fatal illness or debilitating ailment is horrible and there are many events that could lead to our end unexpectedly. Why should any single potential cause of death be faced differently?

After the initial shock of diagnosis, I moved on, put treatments on my electronic calendar so that I didn't have to focus on remembering what needed to be done, and tried to pay attention to the *life* I could live despite the interruptions and effects of the treatments. I preferred to write this book over writing in a diary documenting the experience of illness. If I would die, I wanted to finish this book rather than leave a cancer diary. I didn't ignore the needs of my body, but refused to let cancer invade my spirit. My spirit felt well. It helped me confirm its potential to live despite the fate of my body. I connected with the metaphor of oil in lamps (Matthew 25) and I feel that my lamp has oil. I feel strong in my Spirit and it helps me to know something other than my body. In that sense, I perceive eternal life as strength of the spirit to prevail eternally over the body's temporal limitations.

To me, the promise of paradise is neither an incentive nor a disincentive. I am willing to wait and see. I see those descriptions as an attempt to put into the language of earth concepts that are beyond our experience. It is a promise of good, and my focus is not on the promise, but on life today and how I can live fully on all the planes open to me.

These explanations are just that, explanations, not proof in the historical sense. As I write these words my mind keeps returning to the image of a baby in the womb and how incredulous it would be to tell him of the world that awaited him ahead. His vocabulary and experience are limited to the amniotic fluid, the muffled sounds through the walls of his mother's womb, stomach gurgles, heart beat and intakes of breath. What analogies could one possibly use to urge him to believe? Fortunately, no one has to. The body is nurtured and propelled into this world.

Depictions of heaven may seem completely incredulous in the face of the caterpillar-like lives we experience. Yet, Christ's presence on earth, his death and resurrection are described as the first fruits (1 Cor. 15:20), acknowledging its departure from the norm—a reasoned, optimistic explanation, even if without proof-- to rationally dispel that incredulity. It may seem a safe bet to follow Christ and echo Christian doctrine to err on the side of caution. On the contrary, it is the betting, but the exercise of awakening the power of the spiritual 'body' that makes us able to perceive God as real. That awakening comes from God through our sincere choice to follow him.

We have free will and free choice to nurture our spirits for a full experience now and in preparation for experience in another world, or to remain skeptical and let the spirit go hungry. These explanations are presented with empathy for the skepticism, respect for the search for truth and unwillingness to accept platitudes. I feel the life of my spirit and am trying my best to use words to share that with you.

Paulo Coelho told the story of a caterpillar that was helped out of its pupa and as a result, its wings did not have the strength to fly. It turns out, the struggle was necessary for the development of its wings. Similarly, these insights about life after death may not answer all questions, but sharing perspectives may serve as stepping stones for individuals on a walk to their spiritual awakening. This process, though imperfect, is strengthening. The alternative of accepting the belief in God as the lesser of two evils and out of simple fear of being wrong may deny the spirit the benefit of struggling through the angst of disbelief.

Reflect and Explore:

A) Think about your favorite song. How would you describe the music to someone who could not hear? Assume that they possess all other faculties.

B) If the above 'Clues to the Kingdom' give hints to features and characteristics of eternal life, can you identify which features or characteristics are presented in this list? You may list them on the following page, and feel welcome to share on this book's website.

C) What questions do you have about the perspectives of heaven presented in this chapter?

D) Are there particular descriptions that stand out for you?

E) Reflect on the statement in Romans 14:17 that "the kingdom of God is not a matter of eating and drinking, but of righteousness, peace and joy in the Holy Spirit."

F) PERSONAL ASSIGNMENT: Take some time to reflect on your perspectives about eternal life, and any ways that the clues in your list (or the above list) help or hinder your understanding.

My Personal List of Clues		

Chapter 5: Unanswered Prayer

Prayer, "the converse of the soul with God," a pithy definition attributed to Theologian Charles Hodges (Theopeida.com), is approached in different ways by different Christians. One common factor in all approaches is the expectation of an answer: often a positive answer. Unanswered prayer, the term used to describe the experience of praying to God and not experiencing the requested blessing, could be a major obstacle to belief. It is also, no doubt unwittingly, the term that is used when the answer seems different from what is requested.

It is painful to read stories like "Why did God let my child die" and "When my mom was sick, we fasted and prayed for her, but she died." This discussion is presented with compassion for those who cite the healing of Jairus' daughter (Matthew 9) and the Centurion's servant (Matthew 8) as the basis of their confidence in their prayer. Our perception and perspectives could influence our belief in God and his goodness, his faithfulness or even his omnipotence. Does he care? Is he supreme? More poignant: *is he real?* These are questions raised when we perceive "unanswered prayer."

The context that may present the greatest difficulty in the perception of unanswered prayer is:

your Father knows what you need before you ask him.
Matthew 6:8, NIV

Our life – our wellbeing -- is in his hands. It doesn't mean that we won't pray; but that we don't worry about the outcome. To believe this is to believe that prayers are much like a request to a superior, a professional or expert whose care and integrity are respected and deferred to. To feel that the answer reflects a deficiency on his part is contrary to belief in this context. Do you question your doctor's competence when he says no to something you want? If we respect the professionals we consult, we are inclined to accept their answers. If we approach God with absolute trust in his perfection, how could we have any doubt whatsoever that his answer (not our request) is absolutely perfect for us?

A recent account of the plight of Leslie Nurns (not his real name) came to my attention. Leslie experienced what I can only call a foreclosure blessing. He had a mortgage on his home, and through some error, his bank filed a foreclosure lawsuit against him. Since his credit had previously been excellent, he had confidence in the banking system and was completely unprepared for this turn of events. A servant of God, Leslie also felt at that moment that God had deserted him. How could a loving God allow this financial disaster to befall his child? Still, Leslie did not give up and fought the foreclosure lawsuit. Unrelated to the suit, Leslie's income and financial strength also unexpectedly took a serious turn for the worse. The economy soon experienced a general recession.

Soon, Leslie realized that had the bank not made the mistake, he would have defaulted on his mortgage because of the impact of the recession, and would have had no defense against the foreclosure. However, because of the bank's mistake, Leslie was blessed with a reprieve. While others were losing their homes, Leslie began to see the unjust foreclosure as a blessing that gave him reprieve during the unrelated, unforeseen declining economy.

Like Leslie, we cannot see the road ahead. Sometimes what seems to be a disaster can put us in a better position to face tomorrow. The Genesis account of a family of brothers who attempted to destroy their father's favored son, Joseph, is one example. Joseph's response to his brothers' cruelty offers us a faithful response to the challenges one encounters in life. Joseph said to his brothers:

> *You intended to harm me, but God intended it for good to accomplish what is now being done, the saving of many lives.*
>
> *Genesis 50:20 (NIV)*

Years after suffering because of his brothers' jealousy, Joseph was in a position to help his entire family and save his people from famine. So too, when circumstances arise and our prayers are unanswered, however painful it may be, we can assume that God's purposes extend beyond our immediate circumstances. We must consider whether what we perceive as unanswered prayer is an answer that comes with God's superior judgment and righteousness.

That benevolence in an answer to prayer, since it pertains not to yesterday but to the future, may be similarly imperceptible in the immediate timeframe. It took Joseph years before the famine; Leslie Noms couldn't know immediately that a recession was imminent. It may take us a lifetime. We see only the current time. We also cannot know if the things we pray for could, if given time, lead to other calamities.

When I was diagnosed with cancer, I had been making other plans for the year ahead. I had no idea that I would be facing a year of cancer treatments. My plans did not materialize. As I received the treatments, I was glad that I had not made those other commitments that would have been pulling me to other agenda, compounding my recovery. Instead, I was able to write this book without the pressure of someone else's deadline. I felt blessed and fortunate to be working, doing the work I enjoyed most, yet taking as much time as was necessary to heal.

In those cases, clarity about the answer and its goodness came much later than the calamities. Similarly, we may conclude too hastily that a prayer is unanswered or that the answer is uncaring. Prayers are answered in God's timeframe. With patience, we may witness the goodness of the answer. Viewing prayers through those lenses, one can confidently say that no prayer goes unanswered and no answer from God is without his goodness. When troubled about these things, it may not be easy to think that some future time would reveal that goodness, but perhaps this understanding may help you, even when you can hardly find peace with God's will, to have no doubt that he is real.

Could it be that our own fears drive us to believe that God's answer could not possibly be good? When the answer is "no" -- we are denied a particular request, someone dies or something that we had been afraid of happens -- feelings that God has deserted us are understandable. The evidence of tragedy, illness, death, disasters, and injustice often encourages skeptics to scoff and doubt God's power. I again assert the assurances from the first chapter, to help put fears, tragedy and any circumstance that arises in clearer perspective. In prayer, we remain connected to God no matter what we experience in this life. The issues of illness and death, though agonizing, are temporal and form just one aspect of the broader scope of our lives.

Without addressing anyone's particular unanswered prayer, I can offer a brief inclusive reflection. An attitude of prayer that overlooks particular teachings could lead to misunderstandings. A rounded perspective is presented later in this book

One misunderstanding in declaring a prayer unanswered may stem from confusion about whose power reigns. In this regard, readers of the Bible confidently cite the parable of the persistent widow in Luke 18:1-8 as entreaty to approach God repeatedly, making our demand with the force of our own power, determination and will. However, that would conflict with other prescriptions about prayer in the Bible. Although the Bible does teach different things, they are not in conflict with each other. Repeatedly approaching God with the force of our own will would overlook the recommendation for humble supplication as taught in Philippians:

> *Be anxious for nothing, but in everything by prayer and supplication, with thanksgiving, let your requests be made known to God;*
>
> Philippians 4:6, NKJV

We let our requests be made known to God. Tempered by the understanding of this teaching in Philippians, the parable of the widow and the uncaring judge may be seen instead as a call to remain in communion with God, praying day and night to him, (continually), in the same manner as this widow kept returning to the judge who could resolve her request. In that manner, we constantly maintain our presence with God. As described in Luke, that constant communion holds promise:

> *And will not God bring about justice for his chosen ones, who cry out to him day and night?*
> *Luke 18:7, NIV*

Prayer in this perspective emphasizes an ongoing, repeated presence before God. It is paralleled with the widow's presence before this uncaring judge in the parable, who nevertheless responded to her need. Significantly, he did so *out of fear that she would eventually fatigue him* (Luke 18:5). The teachings in the widow's pleas must be taken allegorically, comparing the elements of the tale with the truths of our living ones: the judge's uncaring with God's goodness; the widow's repeated demands with our supplication; the judge's selfishness with God's benevolence; the judge's fearful inspiration with God's prevenient love. The needy widow approached the uncaring judge repeatedly and he responded from his own concern. In parallel, we too approach God continually, laying our lives before him, in his hands, confident that he has the power to grant our desires. Yet, different from the widow, we know that God has called us to ask for our needs, that he is good, and that he loves us. We recognize when we pray that he is aware of our needs even before we ask and that the response is God's omniscient gift.

When dealing with illness and death, Christians may be discouraged by perceived unanswered prayer. I have encountered more than one case in which believers deny that a particular illness could possibly lead to death. Citing the faith of the centurion whose servant was healed (Matthew 8:5-13) or Lazarus' resurrection (John 1:44), some are inspired to approach life denying death. The truth is, being ill does not mean that God has forsaken us. In previous chapters, we explored the reality of God even in the reality of death. It is not changed or discredited by sad and unpleasant experiences in this life, including death and unanswered prayers for healing or other blessings. To put faith in God and his goodness we need not pretend that those things do not exist.

As caring, loving people, we feel profound pain. It is human to hurt when others die. Those situations can terrify us and could foster doubt about a caring, all-powerful God. Recalling previous discussion in Chapter 1: Eternal Life in Perspective, we need to acknowledge that our biological life is perishable. Illness can remind us of our perishable nature. While illness is indeed horrific, it may serve, for the prudent, as a warning bell and an opportunity to prepare. In contrast, sudden death is a shock to loved ones and denies the departed one the opportunity to make amends. People of faith prepare, living life abundantly, not knowing when the "thief" will come. To deny that illness and death exist would be delusional. Given informed perspectives of human life and death, the question when someone dies, is not "why?". We learned that physical death is inevitable. Similarly, in citing the miracles God performed in saving the Centurion's servant or Jairus' daughter as evidence that God prevents his believers from physical death, we must ask ourselves: where are they now? Having been saved from physical death in those instances, were they forever spared physical death? Those miracles are real, they did happen; but we must also face the reality that at some point, so too did death. We must take time to face our mortality. Belief in God's omnipotent power is neither disingenuous nor delusional.

So, how do we pray when someone is ill? Such prayer follows the teaching from Mark 11:24 that our answer will be granted. That does not contradict the preparatory attitude that God knows what we need before we ask as found in Matthew 6:8.

Similarly, we also pray when someone is facing death, remembering those teachings and rightly asking for healing and other blessings even though we know that God knows our needs. Whatever our prayer, our belief in God's power -- not ours, not the goal prayed for -- is the basis for our confidence about the answer. "Yes" is in God's hands. We submit to God's will, not our own. His is the power and the glory. Prayer during times of illness or death will be addressed further in the section A Rounded Perspective of Prayer.

If God knows our needs and the outcome of prayer is in God's hands, why pray? The answer is, prayer is not only *the asking*. Prayer is also *the connection* with God and the *opportunity* to maintain channels of communication with God and to come before him repeatedly so that he knows you. Remember our definition at the beginning of this chapter that prayer is conversation of the soul with God. I take guidance from Luke 11:13 that God knows and gives to his children. That we may struggle with this should not be discouraging. Genesis 32 provides us the example of Jacob who confessed his unworthiness in prayer, struggled with God and received blessings (Genesis 32:9-29). Daniel 6 teaches that Daniel prayed, giving thanks for days, before he ultimately received an answer. It was in his favor. The decree he was concerned about was overturned in a reversal by the king, and Daniel's enemies succumbed to the fate they had sought for him. (Daniel 6:24). We are similarly told in the Old Testament that Nehemiah communicated with God in prayer for days. (Nehemiah 1:4)

With praise and thanksgiving, Nehemiah did not set a time frame, but ultimately months later (Nehemiah 2:1), saw and recognized the opportunity that answered his prayers.

Even as I describe these instances, I must reiterate that I can offer no formula. The goal is not _e_ffective prayer or praying so that you obtain a particular result, but for prayer that _a_ffects your relationship, so that God will not say "I never knew you" (Matthew 7:23). I do not know *why* God gives a particular answer. My advice is that prayer, that converse of the soul with God, involves considerations greater than the asking.

One such consideration is that however we pray, we need to be mindful of the supremacy of God in our lives. We must carry the conviction that he is our father. Whether we are awake or sleeping, living or dead, we submit our lives to God. Relying on scripture:

> *He died for us so that, whether we are awake or asleep, we may live together with him.*
>
> *1 Thessalonians 5:10 (NIV)*

Given the requirement that we submit to God in prayer, I do not see how there could not be acceptance of whatever is the answer to prayers. Disappointment and sadness are understandable and it is human to feel angry, even perhaps hate, but given these perspectives of prayer, the answer to prayer is no grounds to doubt that God is real and omnipotent.

While I can empathize with those who demand and claim particular outcomes in prayer -- those who believe in the power of hanging prayers on walls, repetitions and timing of prayers, forwarding prayers to particular numbers of people in emails and with the advent of "prayer warriors" -- I don't I rest my belief there. My strength rests in belief in *God's* power and in spiritual communication in prayer. I similarly have nothing to share about praying to statues, heads of churches, or other symbols. I acknowledge that I do not have all the answers nor can I pinpoint exactly what sparks unbelief or disillusionment. I have found, however, that with absolute trust in God, not confidence in human *methodology* over the power of God, there is no unanswered prayer.

Yet, I do not presume to grasp the scope and dimensions of God's grace, kindness and goodness to us when an answer to prayer is given. Different styles seem to "work." [I put "work" in quotes because unanswered prayer is sometimes regarded as prayer that did not "work," although prayer is not merely a strategy to get what you want.] Compare the difference between asking for happiness and demanding a particular lifestyle or a particular job; contrast humble requests for wisdom, patience and understanding with bold declarations of healing or a miracle cure. What is the difference if one believer asks for a specific amount of money, while another, with equal trust in God, defers to offer thanksgiving for gifts already given? Which prescription is correct? Among people who approach prayer differently, I have observed equal feelings of being blessed by God's response. In truth, from the witness of my praying friends, I have concluded that God understands his different children and grants our desires based on *his* love and grace. Praying friends share with me the wonder of blessings big and small: spiritual peace, miraculous healing, money, a spouse's spiritual transformation, a child's deliverance, a glamorous pair of high heeled shoes in the right size. Neither you nor I could capture his munificence in an outline defining how we should pray. Matthew 21 and Luke 11 specifically promise a "yes" answer, one expressly conditional on belief [in God] and the other addressed to his believers:

> *If you believe, you will receive whatever you ask for in prayer.*
> Matthew 21:22 (NIV)

> *...Ask and it will be given to you; seek and you will find; knock and the door will be opened to you. For everyone who asks receives; the one who seeks finds; and to the one who knocks, the door will be opened.*
> Luke 11:9-10 (NIV)

In summary, no prayer goes unanswered, and asking is only one dimension of prayer. Any answer is God's, not ours. Disillusionment arising from the answer may stem from some other perspective or some misunderstanding. No particular prayer systems, methodologies, words or volume make prayer effective. Instead, prayer is offered in ongoing conversation with God, and his will and his grace bring about the response. In that ongoing relationship, prayer is not merely about making demands. Also see the discussion A Rounded Perspective of Prayer in Chapter 12: The Mystique of Christian Connectedness Faith must rest in God's goodness, not in our desires or power. "Yes" and any answer from God come with that goodness.

Reflect and Explore:

A) Reflect with hindsight on "unanswered" prayers you may know of and any later clarity.

B) Did the chapter offer helpful perspectives about different aspects of unanswered prayer?

C) Read and reflect on the words of the Lord's prayer (Matthew 6:9-13) Later in this book, we will examine it more closely for a rounded perspective of prayer.

Chapter 6: Darkly Though a Looking Glass- *Poor Eve*

Eve was wrong to disobey God, but that doesn't mean that Eve's will and not God's prevails. Genesis teaches us that God created man and woman. One interpretation of the text is that Eve caused Adam to commit sin and that God was angry and punished them by chasing them from the Garden of Eden. Yet in the account of creation, we read that God blessed them and instructed them to explore the creation:

> *[28] God blessed them and said to them, "Be fruitful and increase in number; fill the earth and subdue it. Rule over the fish in the sea and the birds in the sky and over every living creature that moves on the ground."*
>
> *Genesis 1:28 NIV*

Having issued this instruction from the beginning, it seems logical to deduce that God *intended* Adam and Eve to eventually develop the adult human awareness that would lead to their recognition of their nakedness. Because of my belief in an all-powerful and all-knowing God, it is difficult to believe that God did not *intend* for Adam and Eve to eventually be ready to embrace their biological capabilities, have sex and *increase in number* as instructed in Genesis 1:28.

Secondly, Genesis 1:26-28 tells us that God wanted them to *rule*. How could they rule without knowledge and the ability to assess good and evil?

Even more compelling to me is that God made man and woman with physically complimentary bodies and the ability to reproduce. It is true that we humans do not clearly understand the full scope of God's purpose. Yet, if we do believe that he created us with all our human capacities, and we trust that he never makes mistakes and truly knows every hair on our heads (Luke 12:7), then we cannot question his intent or doings.

In the infancy of their creation, Adam and Eve were instructed not to eat of the fruit of the tree of knowledge. Yet, immediately after Eve was created and Adam greets Eve, we are told:

> [24] *That is why a man leaves his father and mother and is united to his wife, and they become one flesh.*
> *Genesis 2:24, NIV*

We do not know how much time elapsed before the incident with the snake, but clearly Adam was already destined to become "one flesh" with Eve, uniting with her as his wife. Concepts of mother and father are immediately part of the story, which, since he had been *created,* would be alien to Adam's experience. Leaving father and mother is also predictive, even anticipatory, of the journey out of Eden. This account in Genesis 2 is consistent with the instruction in Genesis 1 that from the beginning, God intended that his creation would not only multiply but also go forth.

I say "poor Eve" because, before she has a chance to speak, the sin for which she shoulders blame for the rest of time is decreed. It is by God's design (Genesis 1:28), not Eve's, that creation would multiply. Genesis 2 ends with Adam's response on his first meeting with Eve.

By Genesis 3, Eve is confronted with the" "serpent." Although the two incidents are consecutive, there is no indication that they occurred immediately. It is possible that some time elapsed. However, this is arguably a matured Eve who knows the rules of forbidden fruit well enough to explain them to "the serpent:"

> "We may eat fruit from the trees in the garden, but God did say, 'You must not eat fruit from the tree that is in the middle of the garden, and you must not touch it, or you will die.'"
>
> Genesis 3:2-3 (NIV)

I use quotation marks for the serpent because at the beginning of the account, this serpent *speaks*. Significantly, while the serpent speaks to Eve, Adam says *nothing whatsoever*. Yet we are informed that he was right there. Some may say that this has all the elements of a perfect allegory for seduction, with the serpent substituted for Adam's temptation, a conservative shield of Adam's guilt, sin, complicity...

Whether one believes that there was indeed a serpent who spoke or whether that part of the account is a conservative cover does nothing to negate the account of creation. The words convey the same truth using different techniques of reporting.

After God finds that Adam and Eve have discovered their nakedness, he curses the serpent and the ground, but treats Adam and Eve with the compassion of a parent. We are told: "God made garments of skin for Adam and his wife and clothed them..." Genesis 3:21. They were ready for life outside the home Eden. God told them both what to expect with regard to childbirth, work and self-support.

Recalling that in Genesis 1:26, God's quest was to make man in his image and likeness. Genesis 3:21 voices confirmation that Adam was both in image and likeness, like God:

The man has now become like one of us, ...
Genesis 3:21 NIV

In my assessment, this dispels the theory that God had not accomplished what he set out to do. Deep conviction that God is all powerful and omniscient leads me to believe that God's purpose was accomplished. It is difficult to believe that

God did not expect Adam and Eve to eventually acquire knowledge AND that God made them in his likeness.

The account in Genesis also tells us that God created the earth and trees in such a way that they required work:

> The LORD God took the man and put him in the Garden of Eden **to work it and take care of it.**
>
> Genesis 2:15 NIV [my highlights]

The fact that Adam had been working inside the Garden of Eden seems to dispel the proposition that Adam was being punished by a life of work outside. Instead, the Garden of Eden reads like humanity's womb: a safe place where Adam and Eve were held until they matured and were ready for the world outside-- a microcosm of the wider world, including kinds of plants, trees, animals and work that Adam would encounter in the wider world. The omniscience of God and His perfection mean to me that the birth of this whole wide world was his plan, not an accident of Eve's disobedience. It suggests to me that God did not create one man and one woman and plan to have them remain alone, innocent, in the garden of Eden, possessing all the marvelous capacities of the human body, yet not needing to use them. Reading Genesis 2:24 and 25 together suggests the two were *intended* to be man and wife, but were yet unaware of their bodies:

That is why a man leaves his father and mother and is united to his wife, and they become one flesh. Adam and his wife were both naked, and they felt no shame.

Genesis 2:24-25 (NIV)

Based on these verses, I believe that God made no mistake and that the Garden of Eden was not intended to be a perpetual haven. That statement captures his intent that they would leave and that Eve would be the reason. Although God warned his creation about the tree of knowledge, there had been no warning about the serpent. God loved his creation and expressed satisfaction that they were made in his image. He gave them clothing, [Genesis 3:21] and as He let them out of the garden, explained to them what they would find in the world outside [Genesis 3:19]. God explained to Eve about motherhood [Genesis 3:16] and instructed Adam about survival in the wider world they would encounter [Genesis 3:18].

The Bible warns us to beware of false doctrine. {Hebrews 13:9] Limited by human experience, we can make the well-intentioned mistake of coloring the readings with our own emotions. Nowhere in the account of the banishment from Eden does the Bible tell us that God was angry with Eve or Adam. An examination of thirty-two translations uncovers the expression "send forth" or "send out" in the accounts of this narrative in Genesis 3:23. For example:

> *therefore the* LORD *God sent him forth from the Garden of Eden to till the ground from whence he was taken. So He drove out the man; and He placed at the east of the Garden of Eden cherubim and a flaming sword which turned every way, to keep the way of the tree of life.*
>
> *Genesis 3:23-24 (KJ21)*

Expressions found in at least fourteen translations include perspectives such as "expelled," "banished" or "forced" in accounts of that narrative. For example:

> *So the* LORD *God banished him from the Garden of Eden to work the ground from which he had been taken. After he drove the man out, he placed on the east side of the Garden of Eden cherubim and a flaming sword flashing back and forth to guard the way to the tree of life.*
>
> *Genesis 3:23-24 (NIV)*

God made man and woman with the capacity to develop independent thought and action. He watched over Adam and Eve in a confined garden, and when Eve acted against his instructions and demonstrated that she was also able to lead Adam, he let them out into the wider world, clothed for protection and with warnings about the adventure ahead. As birds from a sheltered nest must soar on their own wings, parents also nudge their grown children out of their sheltered home after educating and showing them truths about life. I truly believe that the evidence of technological, medical and other progress and advancement demonstrates that advancement of civilization ultimately pivots on the ability of each offspring to find new paths, burst thresholds and unearth hidden truths.

Although our perspective is that discovery is creation, today's discoveries are but hidden truths yet unearthed. As an example, silicon used in today's technologies was always in the sands strewn along earth's beaches, waiting to be discovered and named. Swedish chemist Jons Jacob Berzelius is said to have discovered silicon in experiments he conducted as recently as 1842. Yet silicon is considered the second most abundant element in the earth's crust. Man is blessed with the ability and desire to search and uncover the hidden beauty, wonder and power obscured from our immediate perception.

Work is part of life. As we become ready we will be heralded into each new garden of life.

I call this chapter "Poor Eve," not only because Eve is eternally blamed for a sin, but also because I believe that God in his wisdom wanted this world of people, homes and music, happiness and laughter. It is hard to believe in God's power and still believe that he did not want this world: that all he intended was a garden with just two people, and that Eve changed the course of God's plan. Look at the options God had: make Eve barren, make Adam infertile... Why endow them with the capacity to multiply if this carnal world was not intended? Opening the door between the garden of Eden and the wider world occurred after Eve reached out and took the fruit of knowledge. My human feeling is that God's heart bursts with pride and joy when humanity prospers, advances, finds and puts to good use the treasures God has sprinkled right under our noses, just within our reach, yet obscured from our immediate horizons.

From Genesis 3, Eve's actions, though prompted by the serpent, were reasoned:

> *When the woman saw that the fruit of the tree was good for food and pleasing to the eye, and also desirable for gaining wisdom, she took some and ate it.*
>
> *Genesis 3:6 NIV*

Eve was able to assess that the fruit was good for food. Notably, she recognized that it was *desirable* for gaining wisdom. Eve felt ready to gain wisdom.

Discoveries such as radio waves that were always present in our atmosphere, yet invisible to our senses, are harnessed within technology in use today. Many treats and truths remain hidden, waiting to be uncovered by the growing wealth of information we share with each other and bequeath to coming generations. This cannot be denied as we look back at world advancements since the time of Adam and Eve.

To believe that God did not intend man to eventually obtain the knowledge of good and evil is to believe that this world was not to be. To believe so would be to think of God as forever weeping at the population expansion of this world: to deny that God embedded within us the full capacity to thrive in this world and cope with the expansion of civilization. In 1903, when the Wright brothers launched the first airplane, world population was approximately 1.2 billion. When internet protocols were first launched in the 1960s, it had grown to about 3 billion. Just over half a century later, as world population bursts beyond 7 billion, man has harnessed worldwide virtual communication systems using revolutionary internet technologies, all utilizing resources within the immediate human environment.

Whatever we believe about the first man and the first woman, we are witnesses to the process of human population growth and understand that somehow, somewhere, there must have been the first person on earth. Today's scholars disagree about the origin of man but share the understanding that there must have been an origin. Our reasoning helps us perceive such an origin even if we have questions about it.

Genesis declares that Eve set the ball rolling and that she inspired Adam. There are unexplained phenomena and secrets to be discovered. From Genesis, we may conclude that God created a multifaceted world, creating man with the capacity to unearth its secrets and to master the increasing complexity of life. Genesis identifies the first man as Adam, and the first woman as Eve. Agreeably, there is missing information. Even in our own family histories, much of the information might be missing if we attempt to document our family tree history back to its origin.

Apart from the accounts described in Genesis, there are scholarly theories about the origins of man. One definition of theory is:

> *a proposed explanation whose status is still conjectural and subject to experimentation, in contrast to well-established propositions that are regarded as reporting matters of actual fact.*
> *Dictionary.com*

One such theory was the theory of evolution presented by Charles Darwin.

A theory, however fascinating, is only that: an idea or thought that awaits proof. The question about the origin of man will continue to fascinate generations. I believe that one of the truths in the story of Adam and Eve is that God's purpose will be accomplished regardless of our individual disobedience, and that there may be penalties to face for disobeying God's commands.

Whatever an individual chooses to believe, we all agree that there was a beginning. We possess intelligence and knowledge that, if we attempt to dissect it into its rudiments, suggest learning. It is intertwined with our ability to thrive. Yet somehow, having been credited with starting the snowball accumulating this necessary, helpful knowledge, Eve is regarded in interminable disfavor. Poor Eve!

By adopting the "poor Eve" perspective, we are erroneously inclined to take a "poor Judas" or "poor Joseph's brothers" attitude, doubting everyone's wrongdoing. That is inappropriate. In reality, Christian values define right and wrong. Disobedience to God is wrong. In using the Bible as a book of faith, it is important to recall that God is greater than all the individual incidents recorded in the Bible. This discussion is presented, not as a defense for disobeying God or for defying Christian principles of right and wrong, but to encourage dialogue about creation and face issues that skeptics find difficult.

Reflect and Explore:

A) What do you understand about roles expected of Adam as described in Genesis 2:15 and Genesis 3:23 and man's role in the world today?

B) What do you understand from the writings in Genesis 3:6 and Genesis 1:28?

C) What do you understand from God's actions described in Genesis 3:21?

Chapter 7: Dimensions of Truth

Scribes, Journalists and other Messengers

If you visit the Sistine Chapel in Rome, you will find, along with the silencing peace that envelops the hushed crowd of tourists, a humbling, awe-inspiring sense that someone went to painstaking lengths to leave a profound message on the expansive ceiling, to communicate something vital to future visitors. There is deep meaning -- a story -- carefully depicted in the frescos. The sense of profound meaning cannot be missed. Even if one is mystified by the significance or the source, it is clear that an important message is interwoven in those haunting brush strokes that hover above. That gifted artist, Michelangelo, poured his version with talented strokes onto the expansive canvas of the chapel ceilings.

Like Michelangelo, each artist applies favored tools to express himself using his personal level of skill. Empty of ideas and of spirit, the art could hang listlessly, an eternal mirror of that listlessness.

Scribes and journalists likewise apply their talent of conveying meaning through words. Each nevertheless relates his unique version of the same occurrence using his preferred vocabulary, construction, language and detail.

The gospels of Matthew and Luke relate some of the same occurrences in Christ's life. Although they share the same perspective, each provides different accounts. For example, in relating the healing of a blind man, the gospel of Mark (Mark 10:46-52) identifies the man by name and explains the meaning of the man's name, conveying that the blind man, Bartimaeus was the son of Timaeus. Matthew (Matthew 20:29-34), on the other hand, does not identify who the blind man was, but conveys to the reader that the blind man was not alone. He was in company of another blind man. In comparison, Luke (Luke 18:35-42) neither identifies the man nor his company.

Scholars believe that the gospel of Mark was written primarily to gentiles who were facing persecution, while the gospel of Matthew was aimed at a better educated audience who believed in Jesus but might have been concerned about the law. Luke's audience is presumed to be wealthier believers of Jesus and may have been more complacent in their faith.

Although the accounts of Jesus' life are similar, the scribes who wrote them may be perceived within the text. Their circumstances and those of their audiences bring a slightly different hue to the perspectives. Truth is then not a matter of the text itself, since they are different. Truth is also not a matter of the author, since each is also different. Writing is only a medium of communication. Omissions, emphases, inclusions, style and interpretations are a necessary component in the relating of truthful matter. Contrary to legal expectations, there is no such thing as relating WHOLE truth.

Similarly, the creation accounts in Genesis tell the same story with different styles, emphases and detail. The first verses of Genesis 1 are considered to be a poetic text. The same account is retold beginning at Genesis 2:4, using down-to-earth images of creation from humble dust. These nuances are also carried over into the English translations. This evidence is no indication of deceit or fictionalizing, but reflects the influence and stamp of the scribes, artists, journalists and all who depict, teach, report and deliver information. We read text, but it is not sterile. It is rich and alive. Somewhere between the lines subtly wafts the breath of the writer, giving life to the text.

Inspired Texts

Christians believe that teachings and accounts in the Bible are inspired texts. The gospels tell of incidents that were witnessed by the writers who were inspired to document them. They capture the experience of the era of Jesus' life on earth, revelations of things to come and explanations and evidence of predictions in older writings. The older writings, i.e. the Old Testament, document the lives of people of old, historic events, family trees and prophecies and collect the instructions of God and the wisdom of people of ages long gone. I regard it as a collection of writings that allow humanity to hand down to each successive generation those essentially human characteristics that maintain and support human intellect above the biological plane.

Many of the traditions documented in the Old Testament are Jewish. Old Testament scribes document that it was Moses, of Jewish descent, who received the commandments [Exodus 20] that should guide our lives. Similarly, the New Testament documents Jesus' life and his message so that generations of people can learn what happened in those years. In this way, the Bible gives us tools to support our *being*. In contrast, other writings, for example engineering texts, support and explain the technicalities, science and mechanics of our *doing*s. All kinds of writings, media, art and culture pass information on to generations. It is helpful to understand that each contributes to different dimensions of our lives.

Truths of Science and Theory

Even when we don't understand the intricacies of various technologies, we are firsthand witnesses to their existence as we use cell phones, drive complex motor cars and capture occurrences in photos and videos. We share in these marvels and we believe the magic we experience even when we haven't a clue how it works.

Writers of textbooks fail to mention that the facts described, analyzed and dissected existed before they were harnessed in technologies. The movement of sound across distances and time existed before the telephone: even before the telegraph and the talking drum. We simply did not know it, did not know how, and had not yet harnessed it. There is much in our natural environment that we are oblivious to. What we term 'science' is often a condensation of man's discoveries about hidden aspects of the environment in which we live. Scientific truths about gravity did not create gravity. Sir Isaac Newton gave the phenomenon its name, but did not create it. The truth is that gravity was already in use when Sir Isaac "discovered" it. Apple pickers worked with the understanding that their apples would fall down, not up; sheep shearers understood that clumps of wool would fall to the ground; the first time a child tumbled out of his cradle, he learned where the natural forces of nature would deliver him. For bringing it to our attention, the man who put that simple truth into words deserved a knighthood. So too, scientists who identify and document creation elements take discovery ownership with names such as "genome" or "DNA." They all bring helpful understanding to our world.

    Science helps our lives and we must respect the work of renowned scientists that forms a foundation of today's understandings. We must simultaneously recognize that scientists may name but do not *create* the laws on which their discoveries are based. In the same manner that journalists document occurrences based on observations of our society, so too scientists conduct experiments and perform research, trying to make sense about what they observe and write about and apply their findings, often in helpful, new ways. Science has a vital role to play in enhancing our lives.

    When I first heard about the big bang theory, I chuckled in anticipation of a clever, funny prank. Until then, theories I had heard of had names such as the theory of relativity, and quantum theory. Gravity was not called the falling down theory. So, the big bang theory certainly got the attention of my right-side brain, and an expectation of creative, comic postulation. Was I wrong! I learned that scientists do have a sense of humor. It took a while for me to stop chuckling to myself. Whenever I couldn't explain something, I would say, *'There was a big bang; that explains it!'*

    Today, the big bang theory is considered among the leading scientific explanations about the origins of the universe.

In a nutshell, the theory states that heat (or other things) preceded the universe that we know today. At some point, something happened, which scientists likened to an explosion (aka *big bang*) and the universe appeared. The theory does not pretend to be final or complete. Scientists continue to work to fill in gaps in our knowledge about the origin of the universe and other theories have been proposed and developed

In appreciating the value of scientific research and theories, we must understand the difference between *how* and *why*. Sometimes the nuance separating them can be the education of a lifetime. In a very simple experiment to illustrate

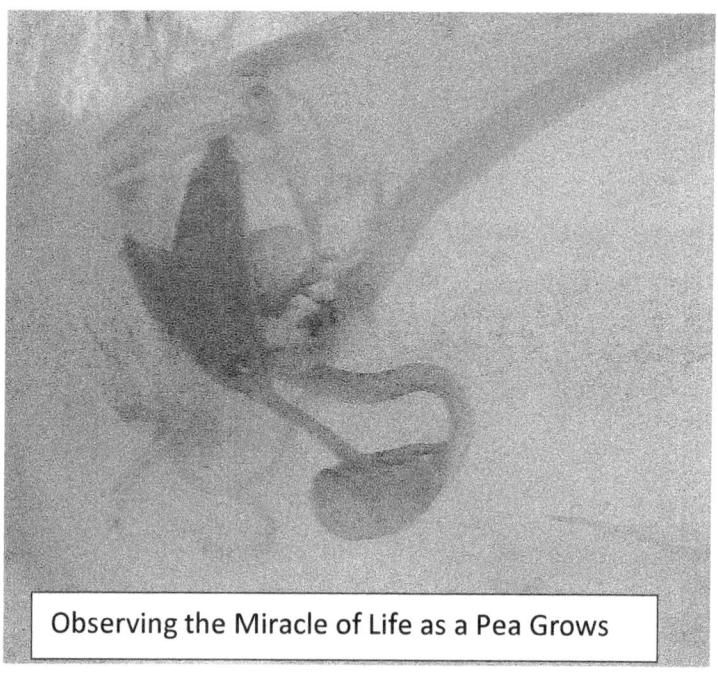
Observing the Miracle of Life as a Pea Grows

this difference, I set some peas in water and watched them over a few days. I observed some changes.

Science Examines God's Creation

Science has explained why these changes occur: the effects of water, sunlight and more are explained, described, proven in scientific experiments. Scientists also explain the value and importance of water and other elements and the resulting effects of deficiencies and this information has proved vital to our understanding of the pea. Who knows, maybe one day they will know enough to genetically engineer a pea. They know it requires intelligence. They have also learned how to modify DNA and fashion genetically similar organisms.

However, the science of a pea did not just "happen". Although I watered the seeds, it was not my choice that some blossomed and some did not. Similarly, science is vital in revealing the miracles of life, including DNA. That is truly awesome. Scientists may also be successful in duplicating what they discover. But it is not those brilliant scientists who *created* what we call DNA and other fascinating truths about life.

Reflect and Explore:

A) What is your understanding of the role of science in perspectives of truth?

B) Considering the discussion in this chapter, what is your understanding about the role of journalists in perspectives of truth?

C) Considering the discussion in this chapter, what is your understanding of the role of the scribes who wrote the Bible?

D) Do these perspectives in any way change the way you use the Bible?

Chapter 8: Essential Truth

The previous chapter attempted to provide a perspective about records of truth. It may be said that a journalist or scribe records realities based on observation and understanding. We similarly read using understanding. When we look for truth, trivial omissions and perspectives aren't necessarily evidence of inaccuracy or falsehood. Instead, we may consider that the core truth remains and is not distorted by certain omissions or perspectives. This is true, for example, in the differences previously discussed about the account of Jesus healing the blind man in the gospel of Mark when compared with the gospel of Matthew. This does not alter the essential truth of the healing and that is reported by three different scribes.

Similarly, when we look at the reports in today's headlines and compare with news on television radio, and other media, the differences do not alter the essential truth that there was an accident, a protest, a birth, a death, although each may report different details.

When Princess Diana died in 1997, Elton John's tribute, "Goodbye, England's Rose" expressed the emotion and sentiments that were shared by many across the world. That artist used his medium -- song -- to capture the sadness of the loss felt by a public that loved her. For me, and I am sure others, the song is forever intertwined with the memory of her death. Yet, the song is a re-worded version of Elton John's twenty-year-old "Candle in the Wind." Although the original was not written for Princess Diana, the use of it twenty years later to express the sentiments surrounding her death does not change the essential truth it represented in 1997. The point is that essential truth is represented using different media and different literary, artistic and journalistic techniques.

This understanding of the way essential truth is presented helps us see words as vessels that contain the 'material' being of the writing. The material is more important than the vessel. This helps us to find truth, not only in different languages, but also interpreted in song, in legend, in poetry, in caricature and other forms of social exchange and communication, as well as in our religious records.

This means that, for example, we need not deny the essential truth that Jesus was born because there is some dispute among historians and archaeologists about the calendar celebration on December 25th or January 6th. We also need not argue about whether the "right" Sabbath is Saturday, Sunday or some other day if we accept the need for Sabbath.

The word 'Sabbath' has its origins in Old English, and means "Saturday as a day of rest." Today some Christians observe Saturday as the day of rest and others choose Sunday. Guidance from the Old Testament is that mercy, not sacrifice, is what is required (Hosea 6). Jesus reinforced this in Matthew 12. That different communities of faith observe different Sabbaths should not be an issue of contention about the essential truths.

The truth of ancestors' input in who we are today is undeniable, though often obscure: for example, traditions of nurture and education, growth and development. As we build our homes, we may not remember who first used gabled or sloped roofs, or even think about the earliest builders from whom the techniques we use were handed down to us. Yet, that does not change the essential truth that someone existed who did.

Similarly, scribes and journalists may record occurrences using their own words, omitting some details. These have been handed down to us in, for example, writings such as the Bible. Each may present different details, yet that does not change the essential truth of what did occur.

Neither evidence, nor lack of it, changes the essential truth. When we do not ourselves experience something, our trust of the source of our information influences our belief. If we trust that a scribe or journalist is not maker of the occurrences they document, we accept their accounts as true. Consequently, as we read the Bible and other books, we must recognize our belief systems and how they influence our responses to what we read. For example, we trust science and regard with respect reports we receive from the scientific community simply because of our science based belief system. We give credence to claims from scientists, because we trust whatever is called science, often whether or not they meet important standards of the science we respect.

In the same light, if you *believe* evolution, you will accept that the chronology proves it and that similarities in genetic composition demonstrate descendancy. Yet, logical analysis shows that no genetic composition nor chronology disproves creation. The conclusions stem from *belief*. In comparison, when subjected to logical analysis, belief in creation does not preclude acceptance of genetic similarities. Science is helping us to understand more about the history and genetics of life forms and their similarities and differences. We gain understanding of more details of God's work.

In court, evidence is used to tell a story. An occurrence that is true takes second place to the story that is told by the evidence. In this way, guilt or innocence is not a matter of *truth* but of *belief* in the story told by presented evidence and witnesses. A witness telling the truth may be disbelieved because of lack of evidence, their mannerisms or even based on some prior incident raised in court to discredit their character. This is so even if they are telling the truth. In essence then, the jury determines what they believe to be guilt or innocence, not truth.

Witnesses in a court of law are sworn to tell "the whole truth." But what is the whole truth? Although it is true that you had eggs for breakfast on the day in question, or that you always enjoy lunch with a knife and fork, this is likely to be omitted from presentations to the court. Hence the whole truth is generally understood as selected facts, not the unedited litany that is the *whole*. Witnesses to the truth edit and report, in their style, facts that present a perspective of truth, omitting snippets of information and embellishing others, unconsciously or deliberately. In a court of law, truth is not absolute, but based on judgment of the evidence both by the witness (who determines what is reported) and by the listener (who processes the evidence through his belief system). We delude ourselves if we think courts have any better access to truth than the access given by belief.

Part of our delusion is the belief that a group of peers would not represent the biases of the individual. Justice is embedded in the responsibility of the judge and in the collective perspectives of peers. We have seen how that works.

As I write this chapter, people across the US are expressing outrage at jury verdicts in two states where a white policeman killed a black man. The collective public protests do nothing to change the decision of the twelve jurists in each case. Public conclusions based on the videotaped evidence seen by the public and broadcast on various media are in complete opposition to the decision of the twelve. Having viewed the same video evidence, these two groups do not have consensus about the verdict.

Another dimension of the reality we perceive as truth is the influence of interested parties. A lawyer may direct questioning in court to elicit discussion of particular facts and to exclude others, so as to shape the 'truth' consistent with his client winning. This means that the realities presented are shaped in some manner, not only by belief, but also by the interests of parties.

These realities about truths we encounter in our lives help us develop a context in which we as rational people can accept the Bible. Although some of the truths are not our personal experiences, we recognize in the writing the Spirit of Truth. It is the same judgment applied to evidence, which we delude ourselves as somehow evaluated by an absolute yardstick-- evidence and witnesses. We will each read the Bible, and some will believe the truth and some will not. Reality is absolute. It can neither be changed nor totally duplicated. In contrast, reports are representation of that reality and fall short of the totality of reality.

The book of Genesis presents the essential truths about the beginning; Exodus about the migration of the early Jews; Matthew about Jesus' life. Some information is not within the record. For example, we are told that Jesus was a carpenter, but no reference is made of any of the pieces he manufactured. Similarly, we wish we knew more detail about the creation, about Bartholomew, and various details to answer some of the questions we have.

Neither in science, nor in law which we uphold as objective, do we have all the answers to the questions that plague us. Some pieces of information are missing. So, the absolute truth and the truth as we know it may not always match. For example, if you look at two different movies about crucifixion of Jesus Christ, you will see the basic story line, but there will be differences. In one, Simon from Cyrene may have Jesus' cross on his right shoulder as he drags it toward the crucifixion site, while in the other it could be on his back or left shoulder. Neither makes a difference to the essential truth of the crucifixion. Based on collective historical records, there is no denying Jesus' birth, life, crucifixion and death.

I remember seeing the movie *The Passion of The Christ* (2004. In it, the producer chose to depict an extremely bloody scene. Most depictions I had seen before then had presented a clean Christ nailed to the cross with a few neat, perfectly pear shaped drops of blood. Yet suddenly, I felt awakened to what seemed to me to be a more realistic depiction—perhaps closer to the truth—that Jesus must have been bloody from the beatings. Even though I believe that version may very well be closer to the truth than the perfectly pear shaped depictions of drops of blood, neither changes the essential truth.

No doubt the traditional depictions were consistent with our social aversions to blood and bloody scenes. Some may want to fault the traditional depictions as concession to social tastes. Others may blame the contemporary producer for sensationalism and unnecessarily bloody depictions. I felt that my understanding matured with the movie. Others may feel differently. What matters is that, although each is different from the Bible versions of the story, they are not *un*truths. They present the essential truths of the crucifixion-- different media, diverse techniques and selected facts.

Indeed, even in the Bible accounts, details of the crucifixion are recorded differently by each scribe. For example, Matthew 27 reports that Jesus was flogged, had a crown of thorns placed on his head, was spat on, mocked and struck in the head. Mark 15 also reports the flogging, crown of thorns, and striking, yet Luke 23 does not mention the crown of thorns. When we read the report in John 19, we also find the flogging and crown of thorns, but the account in this chapter is the only one of the four accounts that reports that Jesus carried his own cross:

> *Carrying his own cross, he went out to the place of the Skull (which in Aramaic is called Golgotha).*
> *John 19:17 (NIV)*

What could this mean? Accounts like these help us to understand the role of the Bible and how we need to read it. Different "reporters" recorded the same stories. Each chapter is a sacred record preserved and translated through centuries and across languages, so that each generation has available a record of the essential truths about humanity—truths from God. No version describes the furniture that Jesus the carpenter built in his lifetime. That was not considered essential for us. An interesting detail, no doubt, but *it does not matter.* What mattered is his message for us. True, Mark did not consider the crown of thorns to be essential, but Mark not only named Simon, but also authenticated his identity by referring to Simon's sons, Alexander and Rufus in Mark 115:21. That John did not include mention of Simon in his account does not mar the essential truth. Simon and Jesus may have carried the cross at different points in the journey. It is possible that from where John stood he might not have seen Simon of Cyrene carry the cross, or didn't regard it as an important detail. Both are speculations. Matthew 27:32 also does not say where the cross was as they were going out, only that "As they were going out they met a man from Cyrene, named Simon and they forced him to carry the cross." Is it important to know if that was the incident on which Matthew based inclusion of Simon in his account of the events?

It is undeniable that Jesus lived and that he left a message for us. The essential truth is the message God wants us to receive. Written by different scribes and translated through the ages, it is preserved for us in the Bible. Our ancestors have done their best to leave an eternal message using simple words like sky, seeds and sheep that they thought we could relate to through the ages. Many speculate about gaps in information, and many scholars today offer explanations and analysis, but we simply do not have all testaments from that time to clarify our speculations.

Reflect and Explore:

A) Are there essential truths identified in this chapter that are meaningful to you?

B) Discuss any criticism you have heard about the Bible

C) Does it fall into any of the following categories?

   Criticism about evidence or proof

   Criticism about missing information

   Failure to match another account

D) Have you identified criticisms outside these categories?

E) Do the criticisms discredit the essential truths of your belief?

PART II

AWAKENING THE QUIET SENSE

Stand firm then, with the belt of truth buckled around your waist, with the breastplate of righteousness in place, and with your feet fitted with the readiness that comes from the gospel of peace. In addition to all this, take up the shield of faith, with which you can extinguish all the flaming arrows of the evil one. Take the helmet of salvation and the sword of the Spirit, which is the word of God.

Ephesians 6: 14-17 (NIV)

Chapter 9: Exposing Misunderstandings

When I began to write this chapter, I had just been diagnosed with breast cancer. For me, the diagnosis was a shock. I didn't feel ill. In fact, I felt fabulous. I was not accustomed to being ill, and the mere thought of facing illness was unwelcome. I had previously accompanied other friends and family along the cancer journey, being part of their support system as companion, encouragement and reassurance. But those experiences hadn't been *me*. I was not the one diagnosed with cancer. At the end of a day, I could put it down, continuing my routines. Now, the thought "I have cancer" constantly runs through my mind, along with "can you imagine!" and simply "wow!" in shock, as I pray and ask God to help me. This new experience has helped me to review and add new perspectives to the understandings I share in this book.

As I considered treatment options, I reflected on God and His healing power. Christians facing serious challenges often turn to God. It is my belief that turning to God should not mean that contemporary help should be excluded. God's intervention is not necessarily the unseen granting of a wish or prayer. Yes, that would be nice to have. But we and others may participate in the answer to our prayers, by giving of our gifts and talents. There are other nice to haves that I will address in turn.

Illness-free Life

One Christian 'nice to have' is an illness- free life. The question is often asked: if God is real, how come God's people get sick and die? Belief that God is real is not about Christians remaining disease free. I have known since I was ten that one day I would die. I could hardly read of a fatal accident or illness or some killing without recognizing that that person once lived, once had hopes and dreams, laughed, loved, cried, and perhaps visited marvelous places, enjoyed spectacular vacations and experienced the wonderful joys of this life. I have known that one day, whether by accident or illness, I too would succumb to my human condition.

Some time ago I published the poem *That Left Home This Morning:*

> *THAT left home this morning too,*
> *It was a person then,*
> *With plans and hopes and things to do…*
> *Senseless accident,*
> *   Or purposeful stroke of eternity's pen*
> *   Writing each life, organizing our time so that we know not WHEN?*
> *©Karen Sinclair, reprinted from the book Jungle Heart (1992).*

My faith in God is within the context of that knowledge and is unaffected by the cancer diagnosis. My uncertainty is about what steps I should now take, and how to avoid all the hype surrounding this disease. I want to finish this book. I believe that God is with me as I write and I would like to do His will. Why now? I don't know. I trust that every experience I face in this life will be used by God for His purpose. Even when illness is not fatal, it takes time to take care of it. Normal schedules are interrupted with treatments, therapies, testing and their side effects, as well as the effect of the illness itself. My hope is that I will continue to write, as I still don't know what will happen tomorrow, or even later today. My faith is expressed in continuing to live and continuing to write as I get help to deal with the disease. I have used medications to fight colds and to cure a stomach ailment and doctors have helped me through various minor sicknesses, prescribing solutions that have improved my quality of life. Similarly, I have confidence that there may be doctors who can help me to overcome this cancer. That's their job. My job is to write and I will continue to do so until I can't.

Death Penalty

Wouldn't it be nice if God would save our bodies from death? That whenever we get ill, we would recover? People often ask why bad things happen to good people. The answer is that things that happen aren't about the people they happen to. All events and occurrences are not penalties and tolls, determined by whether the person is good or bad. Although we have free will to do as we please, occurrences other than our doings are not in our hands. I want to live and don't want to have cancer, but the occurrence of cancer is not in my hands, nor is death. I have done and am still doing the best that I can to take care of the aspects of my life that are within my control, including diet, exercise and a healthy lifestyle. Yes, I've sometimes not done or eaten or exercised as I should. It might have been nice to see events and occurrences as if they were penalties and tolls for good or bad actions. Then we could keep our acts pristine and live without illness. That is simply not what life is. Life is about facing whatever comes. When the ball is in your court, play it with as much skill and energy as you can muster. Play a good game, exhaust yourself in the process, and enjoy. Trusting God, place your life and death in his hands.

This world and everything in it belongs to God (1 Corinthians 10:26). Instead of a penalty, death is a passage to another of God's mansions. We are told (John 14:2) that there are many in God's house.

Many people arrive at the notion of death as a penalty for sin from the statement in Romans that "the wages of sin is death." However, when one looks at the full statement, one can recognize a different message:

> *But now that you have been set free from sin and have become slaves of God, the benefit you reap leads to holiness, and the result is eternal life. For the wages of sin is death, but the gift of God is eternal life in Christ Jesus our Lord.*
>
> *Romans 6:22-23*

Those verses assert that God's people have been set free from sin and the permanent death that results from it. Their wages as slaves of God are eternal life. To express this another way, even though we all face death, we have the opportunity to live in Christ. Human death is not the final destiny of those who live for God. The death of the body does not prevent eternal life, and thus is not a penalty for sin. The death that prevents eternal life is the wages of sin.

Everybody dies, sinners and saints, but scriptures tell us that not everyone rises into eternal life. Only sinners *not* reconciled to God receive that penalty. Instead, we all die with either the gift of eternal life as wages for being slaves to God, or the penalty of eternal death for sin. God is always within our reach to comfort and heal us during this perishable existence in which pain and suffering prevail. He is also near when we die.

Misperceived Limit of God's Power

Aligned with the notion that death is a penalty is the notion that God is absent when there is pain and suffering or that we experience pain and suffering because it is beyond God's power. People base this conclusion on several verses in the Bible, including:

> *The Lord is good to all; he has compassion on all he has made*
>
> *Psalm 145:9 (NIV)*
>
> *For everything God created is good, and nothing is to be rejected if it is received with thanksgiving*
>
> *1 Timothy 4:4 (NIV)*
>
> *For the LORD God is a sun and shield; the LORD bestows favor and honor; no good thing does he withhold from those whose walk is blameless*
>
> *Psalm 84:11 (NIV)*

And more frequently quoted:

> *... all things work together for good to those who love God,*
>
> *Romans 8:28 (KJ21)*

These statements are all separately and collectively true. But they do not provide the full perspective. The way to read the Bible is to understand that although everything is true, the Bible is never contradictory. Each statement provides a careful dimension of meaning. In that sense, although all good comes from God and he is our source of goodness, we must simultaneously recall Isaiah 45:7, that:

> *I form the light and create darkness, I bring prosperity and create disaster; I, the Lord, do all these things*
>
> Isaiah 45:7, NIV

That statement that light and darkness, prosperity and disaster are all from God is another important dimension to consider. God is indeed good to us. If we put our lives in God's hands and accept Him as our Lord and savior, it is not that "good" things come from God and "bad" things from somewhere else. Instead, our whole life is in God's hands if we believe, including any pain and suffering. All things, good and bad, will work together for God's purpose. Although things may *look* bad, ultimately, there is a good outcome.

Many leaders of Christian faith speak only of the good from God, and it is indeed comforting. I understand people who need to see God's power as limited. In taking all the truths in the Bible together, we cannot accept the truths of his goodness and deny the specifics of the story of Job. Whether allegory or chronicle, the account specifically relates that God drew Job to Satan's attention (Job 1:8-12). Job had accepted God as his salvation (Job 1:8) and in the final analysis he was rewarded by God (Job 42:12-16). We are also privy to the taunts of Job's friends, Job's stoic trust in God, and the wisdom of the young Elihu who advised:

> *For God does speak—now one way, now another—*
> *though no one perceives it. ...*
> *Or someone may be chastened on a bed of pain*
> *with constant distress in their bones, ...*
> *From Job 33:14, 19 (NIV)*

In a nutshell, the wisdom from Elihu is that human pain is wrapped in the mystery of God's power and purpose. Elihu points out in Job 34:10-15 that it is unthinkable for God to do evil, since all humanity would perish if he did. Citing God's mysterious and unfathomable power, Elihu voices the understanding that we are just too limited to attempt to understand God's reasons in the grand scheme of the wonders of the world:

> *Who can understand how he spreads out the clouds,*
> *how he thunders from his pavilion?*
> *See how he scatters his lightning about him,*
> *bathing the depths of the sea.*
> *This is the way he governs the nations*
> *and provides food in abundance.*
> *Job 36:29-31 (NIV)*

We cannot downplay the power of God. The complex conclusion, taking all these perspectives into account, is that God is never evil: he only does good, and his power extends to all aspects of life, including illness and death. We simply may not understand the reason why any specific event occurs, but we know that God's work is never evil.

Self-healing Body

Another 'nice to have' would be a self-healing body. It is true that our bodies were designed and created with a built-in healing system, including the immune system. Medical science takes advantage of that system to promote healing. For example, the principle behind the use of vaccinations is that if the body is exposed to a small amount of some kinds of disease, the body's natural healing system would have an opportunity to "understand" it and develop an immunity to it. Vaccinations work because the small exposure helps the body to resist encounters with larger, more deadly amounts of the particular disease. God made us that way. This is a natural feature of the body discovered by scientists and incorporated in methods of treating disease.

However, we do get ill, sometimes seriously, and that healing mechanism takes time. The challenge is to keep the body alive particularly during the course of serious illness. Secondly, the healing system can collapse if there is too much disease or if a person is already weak, malnourished or somehow compromised. Thriving is therefore not only about illness and the body's immune system, but also about caring for the body in illness and health. We participate in our physical care. Despite the body's healing mechanisms, our good health demands that we act intelligently in that care using advances in our understanding and techniques.

Early intervention attempts to take a disease away by other means before the body succumbs to it. Intervening with some form of care spares the body the exposure to the disease progression and the chance that it could succumb to it. I do not know if early intervention with an invasive cure robs the body of the opportunity to develop its own understanding and resistance to any particular infection. State-of-the-art medical care in recent years pursued treatment without a review of the body's own mechanisms and whether the body itself was attempting to attack disease. Medical news today is that more treatments are being developed that work in step with the body's immune system. Accepting medical and other treatment is not a denial of trust in God. Although the body does have a healing mechanism, additional help is often needed.

Secularity in Celebrations

Many serious Christians complain that some Christian celebrations have become too commercialized. Leading the list is the celebration of Christmas. Some are offended by the general sense of merry making, shopping, feasting and partying that mark the season of Christmas, often without any reference to the Christ whose birth is being celebrated. Many believe that it would be nice if Christmas could be more solemn, more focused on going to church and more reminiscent of the profound gift of the savoir Jesus Christ.

In my view, such a belief regarding Christmas, though well intended, overlooks one core principle of the Christian faith- the openness and inclusiveness of all who accept Christ into their lives. Strewn throughout the Christian calendar are celebrations only Christians attend. Without the inclusiveness of the celebrations at Christmas, public access to the religion could recede into an obscure mystery. I marvel at the unfathomable power of God, and how this celebration has grown into a worldwide, all-inclusive embrace beyond the boundaries of Christian life and the walls of churches. Christians cannot keep Christ locked away in Christian churches. The universal embrace that the Christmas celebration affords ensures that the spirit of Christ can touch lives everywhere, unexpectedly, effortlessly, beyond church doors. Keeping Christ in church might be nice for some faithful worshippers, but the essence of the Christian faith is that Christ welcomes all. Celebrating Christ is part of Christian life, but it is not for Christians alone.

Human greed, which may be part of the motivation behind the commercialization of the Christmas celebration, therefore serves as a vessel for conveying the message of Christ to the wider world. The message—scattered like seeds-- gives everyone a chance. Although merchants themselves may be motivated by their own profits, choosing Christmas forces them unintentionally to promote trappings of Christmas, and therefore be unwitting messengers of the wonders of God's love. Christmas music makes its way into places that churches never reach, including party houses, bars, clubs, and stores, along with the name of God, Christ, spiritual love and hope for humble souls.

In effect, commerce has become a vehicle for the annual broadcast of the Christian message far beyond Christian associations. His word of love is scattered to grow along the same paths that adverse messages thrive. We can be guided by the explanations in Ephesians 2 that Christ's message is not for an exclusive group of people; and by the parable of the wheat and the weeds in Matthew 13:29-30 that the message is not misplaced in adverse environments.

In truth, Christ's birth is for the unsaved. It is not a private matter. God's will be done.

A Few Good Worshippers

Some believe church is only for the good people of this world. To the contrary, all dimensions of human nature come together to accomplish God's ultimate purpose. Although pious acts may be a mark of devotion, they are not the only acts that support God's work.

Judas Iscariot, whose name is forever linked to betrayal for his role in Christ's death, was also a disciple of Christ. The Bible tells us that Christ knew Judas well and knew that Judas would betray Him. Yet, Christ welcomed him and allowed him to be at the table on the last night He had to spend on earth, had supper with him and included him in the teachings He gave His disciples that last night. Judas was present as Christ discussed the new covenant with His disciples and was included in that first instruction about Holy Communion, despite Christ's knowledge that Judas would betray Him.

Christian associations often seek to exclude different people from participation in Holy sacraments because of various wrongs they may have done or are doing. Well-intentioned Christians do so because they see coming to Christ as a privilege of the holy, pious and good Christian. The truth is that the new covenant is open to all and Christ's table is for everyone who seeks Him. If any judgment is to be made, it is to be *self-judgment*. These instructions were conveyed when Christ explained the sacrament of Communion:

> *So then, my brothers and sisters, when you gather to eat, you should all eat together. Anyone who is hungry should eat something at home, so that when you meet together it may not result in judgment.*

> *1 Corinthians 11:33-34 (NIV)*
>
> *Everyone ought to examine themselves before they eat of the bread and drink from the cup. For those who eat and drink without discerning the body of Christ eat and drink judgment on themselves.*
>
> *1 Corinthians 11:28-29 (NIV)*
>
> *This is my blood of the covenant, which is poured out for many for the forgiveness of sins.*
>
> *Matthew 26:28 (NIV)*

No one is above sin. Someone who dresses in an embroidered robe and elaborate head gear and is called to lead people to Christ can find the same solace in Christ as the unadorned vagrant. At the last supper, Judas sat with eleven other disciples whose sins were unknown to us. Soon after that, Judas betrayed Christ, another disciple denied that he knew Christ and a third doubted him. Later, an enemy of Christ – Paul -- became a fervent apostle of Christ's teaching and served faithfully, doing more to bring others to Christ than some of the others. His service included documenting Christ's life and teachings now included in several of the books of the Bible we use today.

While we do not condone the wrong that people do, how could we be disciples if we only reach those who are already good and saved? Fellowship is not an exclusive right. Further, we may do more for the *purpose* of the church by welcoming any and all kinds of people.

Those notorious servants of Christ are flagrant icons testifying about the all-inclusive embrace of Christ and His teachings. No one is ostracized from the Christian circle. Who has power then to conduct acts of excommunication? Who controls who is eligible for the grace of God and who is not? Recalling that the simple fisherman, the intellectual scribe and the mercenary heart of Christ's first disciples are a pattern of the complex diversity uniting Christian circles in faith, we must conclude that one does not first become a Christian, then begin fellowship with Christians.

This extends to exclusionary membership. One may see those as administrative acts, not acts of God. Relying on writings in Galatians, we learn that in faith we are one in Christ's fellowship:

> *in Christ Jesus you are all children of God through faith, for all of you who were baptized into Christ have clothed yourselves with Christ. There is neither Jew nor Gentile, neither slave nor free, nor is there male and female, for you are all one in Christ Jesus.*
> *Galatians 3:26-28 (NIV)*

Anyone who is turned away from a church for any reason should know that God's amazing grace is beyond human administration. Those who may be discouraged because fellowship in a church seems to have all kinds of criteria should be encouraged that some churches do practice inclusionary worship and welcome all people into fellowship. Just forgive the offenders and move on. Like you, they are imperfect, though perhaps in a different way. We are all imperfect and learning experiences could foster growth of the spirit.

A Hierarchy of Christians

While well-meaning leaders assume the power of God, some well-meaning followers are inclined to worship their leaders. The reality is that Christian leaders guide congregations. It is the role in which they serve, but they too come before God and must answer to Him. 1 Corinthians 12:12 provides guidance for Christians to recognize each as equal, but with different roles in the body of Christ. Leaders study and take vows. In the best leaders, vows are sacred promises, intentions are pure and their hearts are servant hearts. Yet, like each of us, the leaders' journeys will not be complete until they face God. So they, like everyone else, must battle the twists and turns of this earthly life even as they lead others. It would be nice if all leaders were without blemish. That this is not the case is no reason to have doubt about God, but rather to review our worship of our fellow man, even if they serve God in special ways. Maturity of faith requires each of us to build a direct relationship with God and have respect for leaders. Despite their many blemishes, many leaders still fulfil their roles.

Our leaders teach and take us to a place of truth and understanding and we often look up to them. If a leader makes a mistake or commits a crime, it is easy to condemn him and his message, particularly if one has worshipped him. Recognizing that Leaders are fallible, and may require forgiveness, love and understanding, helps the church to function as the Body of Christ. Matthew 23 gives us a warning about leaders who falter:

> *you must be careful to do everything they tell you. But do not do what they do, for they do not practice what they preach.*
>
> *Matthew 23:3 (NIV)*

In other words, leaders are equipped, not with perfection, but with the ability to lead. If we regard leaders in the church with respect, understanding that their role is equally accountable to God, we have the opportunity to scale the hurdle of leaders' faults that may keep us from spiritual nurturing. Leaders may come in all forms; your perspective of their failings is not the obstacle that keeps them from leadership. It is the temptation to worship leaders that corrupts the process. No leader is to be worshipped, even if they wear a gown and a crown and carry a gold staff. Jesus taught:

> *you are not to be called 'Rabbi,' for you have one Teacher, and you are all brothers. And do not call anyone on earth 'father,' for you have one Father, and he is in heaven. Nor are you to be called instructors, for*

> *you have one Instructor, the Messiah. The greatest among you will be your servant. For those who exalt themselves will be humbled, and those who humble themselves will be exalted.*
>
> *Matthew 23:8-12, NIV*

It is not unusual to develop behaviors and practices as we internalize the teachings that we read. Different Christian denominations have over the years developed practices and approaches to fellowship that help to keep people engaged with God. These brand name groups attract people and bring masses to a place where they can learn about God and develop the spirit. They are not to be ridiculed, even if their practices may be difficult to accept. One should also not be confused by the conflict in the different practices and different interpretations of scriptures. Each speaks so that different people may hear and each reaches the different spiritual needs of people of the world.

I identify these dimensions to help those who are daunted by the fanfare. Faith in God is not a cult. You are not required to worship in one particular style in order to find God. God's world is also not only within the walls of a particular church. One also does not have to forego the help of modern medicine in times of illness, nor mingle only with Christians. Neither does one have to be bothered that people do. It is for you to learn the truth. We are all elements that come together with our special differences to accomplish acts of faith. In Romans 12, the Apostle Paul describes that coming together as an act of God's grace to one body:

> *For by the grace given me I say to every one of you: Do not think of yourself more highly than you ought, but rather think of yourself with sober judgment, in accordance with the faith God has distributed to each of you. For just as each of us has one body with many members, and these members do not all have the same function, so in Christ we, though many, form one body, and each member belongs to all the others. We have different gifts, according to the grace given to each of us. If your gift is prophesying, then prophesy in accordance with your faith; if it is serving, then serve; if it is teaching, then teach; if it is to encourage, then give encouragement; if it is giving, then give generously; if it is to lead, do it diligently; if it is to show mercy, do it cheerfully.*
>
> Romans 12:3-8 (NIV)

As part of one body, Christian leaders guide congregations. It is the role in which they serve, but they are equal with other parts of the body of Christ.

Reflect and Explore: (sharing optional)

A) Discuss the 'nice to haves' identified in this chapter, and any others you know of.

B) Identify and list the expectations you have of your faith.

C) Identify and list the practices that are important in your worship life.

D) Reflect on the message in Romans 12:3-8 and any impact it may have on your perception of your role in the church.

Chapter 10: Under the Stand of Faith

Ask a savvy Christian what exactly faith is and you will likely hear a response along the lines of, "faith is the expectation of things not seen," based on Hebrew 11:1. To have faith is to believe in something without looking for evidence of its existence. Faith is a foundation of the Christian belief system and the bedrock for a life believing in God and His existence. Faith is the confidence that we were created and are being looked after and watched over by a creator we cannot see. Faith in God is not a promise that we will get everything we want or that life will be without problems, pain, sadness or death. Faith is that God is here and with me in my life even though I cannot see Him.

Faith is different from a delusionary perspective: a faithful person sees the roses and its thorns, while a delusionary perspective denies the evidence of thorns on the roses. A delusionary person may jump off a roof in folly, while a faithful person will act with absolute confidence that God is always there and does only good, seeks only good, and acts in good faith.

The expression "have faith" encourages a Christian to stand tall and not be afraid of the unknown. For me, having faith means that I allow myself to be guided by and dependent upon God's grace. It is not that I sit and do nothing and wait for God to make life perfect. Not at all. He has given me abilities and I must use them. I will act to the best of my capacity even when it appears that my capacity is inadequate.

Having faith for me is also an attitude. My mindset allows even that when circumstances look bleak, I will not be discouraged. It also means that although negative outcomes are possible, I do not focus on or worry about occurrences that are not within my range of action. However, I do take precautions and act in a sensible manner, knowing full well that there are myriad unforeseen possibilities and that I cannot possibly anticipate everything that may arise.

This may sound easier said than done. I believe that acting with faith begins with a heart of prayer: general prayer that brings mind and body into a condition of peace, connected to God. Prayer from that state is not merely an opportunity to ask and plead for something, but more a place of submission to God, where I can move forward with His guidance and embrace. The ability to do this may take time. Submission requires letting go. I often start with a prayer of thanks, reminding me of God's blessings and the things that are in good order. From time to time, I list different blessings because it is not possible to list them all. This not only helps me connect with the bounty of His provision, but also to be grateful, recognize his blessings and appreciate and use what I have already been given. It also brings me to a place of peace and softness and removes neediness, worry and anxiety.

From this position of prayer, I am lifted up to act, not on my own strength, but through Christ. That is the core I find in Philippians 4:13:

I can do all things through Christ who strengthens me.
Philippians 4:13 NKJV

That verse is for me not about my strength or about what *I* can do. Instead, it is a guiding principle which helps me to change perspective and operate from a core of faith in *Christ's* strength: faith to face the 'here and now' with a confidence and strength that goes way beyond myself and my shortcomings and limitations. Working *through* Christ and *His* strength helps us tap into and benefit from the limitless power of God. For me, letting go and submitting to God is not giving up.

Although this is my approach, I have seen God bless equally the Type A personality who just cannot let go, for whom letting go is tantamount to giving up. God receives us as we are and his blessing is not dependent on a formula.

Like the different beauty found in sunflowers and roses, we each face the world with different gifts. I believe that though different, our gifts are enough for each of us to face the challenges we encounter. Collectively, we won't face challenges completely alien to our abilities, and we need never be alone. From an earthly perspective, God's universe includes some seven billion other people on seven continents and we never need to feel alone or trapped. We also have the world at our fingertips spiritually, since we each can be in spiritual communion with God without flexing a physical muscle.

However, we do feel alone at times, and some situations can make us feel utterly disconnected or trapped without any feasible solution. People we love may hurt us, cheat, desert us, die or fail us in some way. Life's challenges -- including money, jobs, school, health, illness, food, home and relationships with family, friends, the community, legal and other systems -- can build overwhelming weight on our lives. These are not issues of faith and may confront Christians and non-Christians.

In times of need, we can seek spiritual shelter wherever we are in the world. Our gifts and abilities are supplemented by the gifts and abilities of others: in particular, people who assert themselves, stand up and use them. God not only inspires and guides helpers throughout this earth, but he also intervenes directly. Faith that our abilities are perfect and enough means that our days do not pivot on life or death, success or failure, but on doing the very best that we can do each moment. We need not fear anything whatsoever. Live or die, we are free to enjoy milking a perfect day out of whatever we encounter.

Each day provides its own encounters, both positive and negative: crime and goodwill; insults and compliments, mistakes, retakes, successes and failures. Things don't always work as we expect. In short, we face each day's occurrences whether we are blind, bespectacled or perfect in vision: whether lame, able or on crutches. Maybe it is easier if we have perfect vision and both legs, but if we don't, we must embrace what we do have. Fretting about our lack won't do anything about the issues we already face. The day just is. Adopting this perspective, we need not fear outcomes. Scriptures teach us that bad and good will happen. We are *prepared When* we feel that our lives are torn apart, faith moves us steadily forward one stitch at a time, confident as we tear and mend, that the final outcome is not our task.

On Gifted Wings

Moving steadily forward does not mean we should not talk about the issues we encounter each day. Sharing helps us put the day in perspective and may help us clarify and understand what has happened and what if anything we can do. We are equipped to talk about fears and concerns and use what we learn to help us deal with future issues. Our personal gifts are part of a universe of gifts. We noted In Romans 12:6-8 seven gifts of the Spirit: prophecy, ministry, teaching, encouragement, giving, leading, and mercy. These manifest themselves as singing, leading, speaking, listening, teaching, healing, comforting, nurturing, problem solving and other active contributions to the welfare of others.

Typically, no one person is given all these gifts. Also, many gifts remain to be uncovered and even uncovered gifts can sometimes go unused because not everyone steps forward to offer them. Sharing clears the path to the universe of gifts. Jesus described it as a single body working together:

> *Just as a body, though one, has many parts, but all its many parts form one body, so it is with Christ. For we were all baptized by one Spirit so as to form one body*
> *1 Corinthians 12:12-13a (NIV)*

Various obstacles stemming from ourselves or our society, such as discrimination, disunity, disdain and fear or personal and psychological issues, may stifle and obstruct access to and sharing of gifts. It is when we come together that gifts do good, accomplish acts of faith and bear fruit.

To serve with faith, it is helpful to recognize gifts you possess. This may take a few minutes, a few weeks, or a lifetime.

Faith helps us to maintain personal balance throughout situations of chaos, throughout the journey of life, even facing death. We are also blessed with fruit nurtured by that faith. The "Fruit" includes a crop of peace in the world. As expressed in Galatians 5:22, this fruit blossoms from the Spirit, including love, joy, peace, patience, kindness, goodness, and faithfulness, gentleness and self-control.

ILLUSTRATION 1: The Fruit of the Spirit

Based on Galatians 5:22

Various gifts and talents, channeled to the world through different people, help to bear the fruit needed to feed the world both spiritually and literally. In every sense, we are not alone either in our suffering or in our joy. But it is a journey to feel that sense of security and faith. Understanding that no one is alone is progress in the journey.

Together, all the gifts and fruit of the spirit work for the universal good. Sometimes our fear is due to feeling incompetent or incapable. We may feel afraid about the unknown, about results and outcomes that we cannot control. The strain and stress of struggle and the pain of illness may cause us to lose faith that there is a God who could save us. We may lose faith when an outcome seems to be unfair or disastrous, or when there is death. Yet, to have faith is to focus not on the disaster, but to reach out to the unlimited power of God and his gifts universal. That ability, that faith, is also a gift from God. (1 Corinthians 12:9). I was inspired by the Archbishop of Canterbury, The Most Rev. Justin Welby, who said in January 2015 during an interview to Trinity Wall Street, Christians share responsibility to engage with struggle. Faith to engage in the struggles that confront us is not about proof that there will be a particular outcome. It is our mandate to bring our gifts to the world. Faith is reflected in our relying on God as we pursue that mandate. Knowing that God is mighty over all, we can feel confident to step forward to play our part and also be at peace throughout this process.

Faith Without Works

The statement that faith without works is dead is sometimes used as a rebuke based on the words in James 2:14 and onward:

> What good is it, my brothers and sisters, if someone claims to have faith but has no deeds? Can such faith save them? Suppose a brother or a sister is without clothes and daily food. If one of you says to them, "Go in peace; keep warm and well fed," but does nothing about their physical needs, what good is it? In the same way, faith by itself, if it is not accompanied by action, is dead.
>
> James 2:14-17 (NIV)

Faith is unshakable confidence in the unseen. It is the absolute certainty that God exists, that we are not alone and that God is omnipresent and omniscient. Faith never changes and never has doubt. (Faith and lack of faith are like illness and health.) Some leaders rebuke congregations for lack of faith demonstrated by failure to act, while other believers do things to prove that they have faith. Yet the reality is that faith comes from God. (I Corinthians 12:8-9). Since it is a spiritual gift, we must turn to God to possess it. (Romans 10:17) Jesus showed compassion when his disciples lacked faith (Matthew 8:26) and helped them in their fear. This suggests that people can be nurtured toward a life of faith, but it may be putting the cart before the horse to force people to act to prove that they have faith. Instead, leaders observing lack of faith need follow the advice in Romans and teach more about God.

We do not earn salvation *through* our deeds. We also do not earn it by *claims* of faith. Faith does have a role in our salvation which has been given to us by God's grace. Good works are a Christian must, but we are saved by God's grace, not our own acts. Christ has already died, giving his life to save us. Ephesians 2:8 explains that we *have already been saved* and that it is not by our works:

> *For it is by grace you have been saved, through faith— and this is not from yourselves, it is the gift of God— not by works, so that no one can boast.*
>
> *Ephesians 2:8-9*

The words quoted previously from James 2:14 encourage doing good, which is one of the foundations of Christianity. In acts of good, faith becomes visible, alive. As James tells us, faith without deeds is dead. James then teaches them about God. As clarified in Ephesians, salvation is a gift from God, not a function of our deeds. God calls each of us with love. All we have to do is believe. Faith grows and gives us courage to reveal all the goodness within us. Boasting about works or about faith is a different matter. It may be encouraging to others, but for salvation from God, any such claim is moot. Consistent with this, James follows up on his statement with teachings about faith from the scriptures, (James 2:21-24).

People of faith hold two crystal clear truths in their hearts: that God exists and is present and that God is the master in charge of life. They are not oblivious to the spectrum of pitfalls, possibilities and potential outcomes both negative and positive and do not deny the experience of pain, illness and the reality of death and its many shadows. Not at all. Instead, faith gives the courage to face each new challenge with calm and confidence and the understanding that erases worry if and when it surfaces. Without denying reality, people of faith can think and pray and partake in life, knowing that problems exist, yet not daunted by the effort to face them.

Faith is a lifestyle of calm assurance from knowledge of Christ. Combined with practical enlightenment that problems exist, people of faith are not delusional, but are not daunted by the effort to face them. Resources such as prayer connect us with God. He guides our paths and gives us thoughts, talents, ideas, friends and a whole universe of miracles.

So, you *claim* faith by a life of faith. The *life* is the only claim. As we grow to trust in God, faith manifests itself in our lives. A claim (in words only) is not faith itself. As in James' question, what good is such a claim?

In acts of faith, we engage gifts that God has given each of us. We are called to use them and share them. As we do, these gifts manifest themselves in various active contributions to people's welfare. In this way, good has the resources to triumph over every evil in this world. A life of faith provides access to the universe of resources seen and unseen.

Recognizing your gifts may be a step toward understanding a greater plan and where you fit in. I challenge those in doubt to examine their own gifts and talents and those of others. Perhaps as you use your gifts, you will receive new revelations. Although it takes belief in God to put your faith in him, I offer comfort to those who may not believe. It is God who will reveal himself to you (1 Corinthians 2:10).

Reflect and Explore:

A) Reflect on the things that you are thankful for in the life around you.

B) Reflect on the fruit of the spirit and how they are manifested in your community and in your life.

C) Reflect on the message in Romans 10:16-17.

D) Reflect on the message in Ephesians 2:8-9 and what this means for you.

E) Read 1 Corinthians 12:7-11 and Romans 12: 6-8 and consider the gifts in the table that follows. Prayerfully take a few minutes, a few weeks, or a lifetime to assess your spiritual gifts. Use additional sheets if needed).

ILLUSTRATION 2: Assessing spiritual gifts

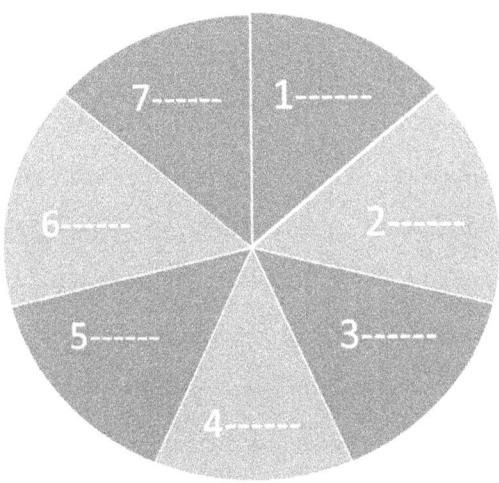

ILLUSTRATION 3: Spiritual Gifts
(Romans 12:6-8)

- Prophesying
- Serving
- Teaching
- Encouragement
- Giving
- Leading
- Showing mercy

ILLUSTRATION 4: Spiritual Gifts
(1 Corinthians 12:7-11)

- Wisdom
- Knowledge
- Faith
- Healing
- Miraculous powers
- Prophecy
- Discernment
- Speaking in Tongues
- Interpretation

Chapter 11: Boundaries of Belief

Quite often, the word belief is bandied about as if it were a commodity on its own. However, belief requires an object. We must answer the question: "Believe what?" or "Belief in what?" In Acts 31, Paul and Silas expressed the words that ring through to us today: "Believe in the Lord Jesus and you will be saved" Acts 16:31 (NLT). They completely whittled away the need for particular actions, sacrifices, activities and rituals, and hoisted salvation squarely on belief in Jesus Christ. How could this be? What does it mean to believe in the Lord Jesus?

Before examining what this means, let us explore what belief is.

What is Belief?

The Merriam-Webster online dictionary defines belief as both a feeling of being sure and as a state of mind or habit. As a feeling, it therefore includes the emotions and senses. As a state of mind, it would incorporate the intellect, and as a habit it can be reflected in behavior, instinct and unconscious or reflex behaviors.

'Belief' is the word we assign to the internal sense about truth: the visceral gut feeling, certainty and personal conclusion that something is true. Including mind, emotion and senses, it is less of a thought process than a conclusion. Think about when someone says, "I believe you," or when you tell someone that you believe them after they tell you something you have no information about. Who can distinguish whether that person's response involves the senses, mind or reasoning? Belief may also be influenced by one's trust of the source. We are more inclined to believe someone we already trust. All these factors unite to create belief.

Demand for proof is often aligned with issues of trust. If one distrusts the source, one is more likely to seek proof. Take for example the assertion that silk is made from threads spun by a silkworm. If you haven't seen it yourself, believing that statement depends on factors including your trust of the source.

In this vein, it is interesting to note that skeptics about God nevertheless believe in doctors and surgeons despite similar lack of proof (other than perhaps belief in endorsements from others). Since the issues of proof are similar, one is inclined to think that the concern is the messenger. Those who do not believe, then, may lack either information or see some other deficiency in the messengers of the belief.

Belief in the Lord Jesus is therefore that certainty in your being that Jesus is the truth. It holds implications for messengers of faith, including the Bible. It precludes doubt and is independent of evidence and explanations about him and his message. It is assurance *about* who he is and the trust *in* what he represents. So, when Christians says "I believe," they are attesting to the certainty they feel, the confidence and assurance that Christ is real. With that perception of belief, we can examine three elements defining Christian belief in God: that Jesus was sent by God, that Jesus is the Son of God, sent for salvation of people, and that there is only one God.

The Belief that Jesus was sent by God

Christ is the foundation of the belief system of the Christian faith. The word 'Christian' is derived from His name. The God of Christ is the God Christians worship. In our society, many other gods are upheld by people, but the God of Christians is the one that created the universe. In previous chapters, we touched on different schools of thought about our origins. Christians consider God, creator of the universe, to be the only God.

Part of believing that Christ was sent by God is believing there is only one God. Christians also believe that God took human form when he manifested himself on earth as Jesus

Christ—born into human life in the way humans are born; growing, walking, talking, eating, drinking, loving, crying, feeling pain and ultimately dying in human flesh. In this way, Christ and God are one. When in the flesh, as Christ the son walking among people on earth, Christ prayed and called upon the father God. United in the spirit, he is one with God.

Belief in One God

Christians worship a triune God. The triune or three-in-one God, also referred to as the Holy Trinity, unifies the ways in which we as Christians experience God. Those ways are as God the Father, God the Son and God the Holy Spirit. That the creator of the universe is the only God is a function of belief. It's quite simple. One either believes that there are many gods ruling over different aspects of reality, or they aren't. In that sense, belief is a conviction. There is no hard proof that we can sense with eyes, ears, touch, taste or hearing of either the truth or falsity. There is only conviction, belief: that intangible sense for which science yet has no tool to define. No debate can absolutely resolve whether there is one omnipotent God. It is a belief: one that is a foundation of Christianity.

Since the quest of this book is not only to explain why I know that God is real, but also to help people over their obstacles, I will also share with you some of the rationale for accepting this Christian view of God. Psalm 115 shares that statues of gods are all manmade. Whether made of wood or gold and silver or whether expertly crafted, they nevertheless are manmade. Those who worship a statue are worshipping a manmade idol. Why?

The same question would apply to the worship of men. Whether they are appointed by groups of respected elders or wear the richest headgear and clothing, their glory is nevertheless manmade. They may hold positions of leadership and possess deep understanding of scriptures, but they are not gods to be worshipped. Their glory is assumed with the position they occupy and may be well meaning and for good purpose, but they are not God. Your relationship with God is not a political one dependent on popular determination, but an eternal one to last beyond the temporal reign of the latest appointee.

To be clear, there is nothing wrong with hierarchies within Christian denominations. The concern is worshipping select members of that hierarchy. We need teachers, who we must accord civil respect, and we all need each other. The truth is, the position of intercessory was abolished by Christ. We each need only be taught about the direct connection to God that is open to us. Of course, intercessors may be welcome when the spirit is broken or too weak, but it does not require pomp and ceremony. Similarly, a member of the Body of Christ may intercede when leaders need help.

When visiting churches, one may encounter some of the symbols of the Christian faith. Among the most frequently encountered is the cross. This is symbolic, and a reminder of the way Christ gave his life and opened one of the many mansions in God's house. The empty cross is a symbol and a reminder of that doorway, endeared, but not to be worshipped or bowed to. There is only one God who can hear and see and respond to your needs and prayers. Among the first commandments decreed, Christians are instructed:

> *You shall not make for yourself an image in the form of anything in heaven above or on the earth beneath or in the waters below. You shall not bow down to them or worship them*
>
> Exodus 20:4-5, NIV

Our prayers go to God, not to a cross or a priest, or even the most beautiful statue of the most respected historic figure; not to any holy elder, living or dead, but to God. Sometimes without intending to, people worship their job because of its place as a foundation of their livelihood. Similarly, factories or animals that may serve as important to the livelihood of a community may seem to be deserving of reverence. Those may indeed provide physical sustenance, but what power could they have over the human psyche, mind and spirit when they must be nurtured, fed and controlled by humans?

Christians believe in one God. Many prophets are documented in the Bible and Jesus' disciples have left profound messages and important documentation about Jesus' life on earth. However, despite their everlasting writings, disciples are not to be worshipped. They too refer to only one God. Others may have made and may continue to make lasting contributions to Christianity, but no saint, no prophet, not even an angel is to be worshipped:

> *I fell at his feet to worship him [the angel]. But he said to me, Don't do that! I am a fellow servant with you and with your brothers and sisters who hold to the testimony of Jesus. Worship God! For it is the Spirit of prophecy who bears testimony to Jesus.*
>
> *Revelation 19:10 (NIV)*

The Bible speaks against worshipping any idol, symbol, animal, saint, angel, disciple or prophet, living or dead. Life has many realities and questions that we as humans can think about, but not answer with science: could there be many little or big gods responsible for different realities? Is there a saint that could offer us protection, or an angel I could pray to instead of God? Is there any God, or is the reality of life independent of a deity? Did amoebae or some living cell just spark itself out of nothingness and metamorphose into varied, well ordered, reproducible, biological life, with lymphatic systems, matching pairs of hands, bone, muscle and flesh of different constituents? Then another amoeba springs a similarly symmetrical organism compatible with womb or sperm? Personally, I find that harder to believe.

There are no photographs or eye witnesses, no records other than those inspired writings some time after the occurrences. Very simply, our answers come down to belief. There are those who believe and those who do not. I believe in one God, follow the wisdom of the Bible and do not offer prayers to any idol, animal, saint or prophet, living or dead.

Belief in The Son

Extending from that belief is the belief that that God, omnipotent creator almighty, had a son... not just *any* son, but a human son, Jesus, who was God's divine persona in bodily form. In that human son, God had a visual, tangible, audible, physical presence on earth. He had friends and did humble tasks such as washing feet and providing wine at a wedding banquet, as well as brotherly scolding of his friends for lack of faith and later for their human inability to keep watch with him at night. Although Jesus was their human friend, his friends recognized and responded to his divine nature. He was apart, revered and supreme, yet brother, teacher, leader and friend. The concepts of God's omnipotence and his son Jesus are intertwined in the

Christian belief. Jesus is the earthly presence of God, not a separate God.

Understanding his presence as a God in human form, helps us to understand how he could die in human form, yet come alive again. The Christian belief in Jesus as the Holy Ghost stems from this.

Belief in Salvation

Another dimension of Christian belief is that Jesus' life on earth and his death were for the purpose of our salvation. We asserted above that believing in the Lord Jesus requires that we believe that Jesus was sent by God, and that his life on earth and his death were for the purpose of our salvation.

Salvation may be defined as the act or means of protecting someone from harm. Theopedia, an encyclopedia of Biblical Christianity, defines salvation as:

> *the act of God's grace in delivering his people from bondage to sin and condemnation, transferring them to the kingdom of his beloved Son (Col. 1:13), and giving them eternal life (Romans 6:23)—all on the basis of what Christ accomplished in his atoning sacrifice. The Bible says we are saved by grace through faith; and that not of ourselves, it is the gift of God (Ephesians 2:8).*
>
> *www.theopedia.com*

There is evidence to believe that someone called Jesus Christ lived and died. Many people have lived and died. A practical, reasoning person would not doubt that someone with that name did exist. That Jesus is a sanctified son with a purpose… that is a hurdle that is crossed with belief.

Scaling that hurdle requires something beyond the evidence that courts of law demand. Unsubstantiated belief can be compared to inexplicable feelings of love. If you have experienced love, whether it is of a child, parent or someone you have met, you have had the experience of which there is no physical proof. We have one word—love: parallel to belief and to the scientifically unsubstantiated knowledge that Christ's life and death were for our salvation.

Belief is not about science any more than love is. Both may perhaps be demonstrated in physical acts. Yet both are undeniably inspired by something beyond us. For those who believe the Bible, we are told in Hebrews 10 that God promised to write his truth in the hearts and minds of his people:

> *"This is the covenant that I will make with them after those days, says the Lord: I will put My laws into their hearts, and in their minds I will write them,"*
>
> *Hebrews 10:16 NKJV*

The truth written in our hearts and minds cannot be denied on grounds of scientific deficiency. We may seek evidence and ask for tangible proof in the quest to use science as a measure of reality and truth, yet lack of proof is not the same as falsehood. A reality check is only that—a check with proof or documentation. It does not disprove the truth.

These dimensions are key to Christian belief in the Lord Jesus Christ and his salvation. It is not a singular belief. It is the belief that Jesus is real in the Christian sense: that he was the earthly son, a manifestation of a singular divine God, and that his life on earth was for our lives. It is a belief bound by understanding and trust.

Trust is also a boundary to belief because elements of Christianity have been undermined by a few leaders' exploitation and greed over the years. Shrewd people develop skepticism from observing deception as people are called to pay for salvation in one form or another. Some forms of deception are blatant. Even with good intentions, a well-meaning leader facing desperate survival needs can be led astray by exploiting people's needs and fears in the effort to survive. In addition, the church is not immune to invasion by leaders with greedy, self-satisfying intentions. The creed "the church must live" opens doors that raise levels of skepticism in what the church represents.

The four lines of the refrain of the well-known hymn "Because He Lives" capture the essence of what it means to believe in Christ. It also helps us to understand the advice from

Paul and Silas to "Believe in the Lord Jesus and you will be saved" Acts 16:31 (NLT). Our salvation comes from God through Jesus Christ, and there is no price but the belief that it is so. There is no price, no tithe, no bribe, no further sacrifice, no payment, no lighting of a candle, no membership dues to earn that salvation. Those contributions may help church operations, but they do not save your soul. Hebrews 10 explains clearly that Jesus' life was the last sacrifice. Believing that is the only ticket to inheritance of his legacy and promise.

To *say* that you believe is different from actually *believing*. It may be uttered in words, but belief is a full conviction of the self, spirit, and heart. It is not about eloquence, piousness, or charitable contributions. Belief has no doubt *in* Jesus and the totality of what he represents. I can't tell you if you believe or if you don't. Only you and God can, and if you do believe, you will be saved.

I believe that all you need to do is to believe. For some people, that belief may lead them to specific acts: dedicating their lives to saving some vulnerable group or committing themselves to some other sacrifice or prayerful reclusive behavior. Those acts are good in themselves, but they are not *requirements* for salvation. The requirement is belief. The qualification is God's grace. It is not *earned* by good acts. True, belief may lead us to do a variety of good, but it is the belief itself that leads to salvation.

Belief leads us to prioritize meaningful living ahead of pleasurable desire. Belief in Jesus does not mean that we stop being human. God made us with pleasurable bodily systems, senses, and nerves. He gave us beauty and love, laughter and fun, music and song, creativity and art. Life on earth without the beauty of sight and hearing, excitement and pleasure would be a denial of our God given humanness, a death. I believe that when our spirit believes in God, our focus shifts. We overcome urges to lie and cheat, because the things that are important never require it. We learn to tell the truth and let the chips fall where they may. By extension, courage develops to speak up when there is need to do so, because there is nothing important to lose when what we need is coming from an incorruptible source.

Some people may follow a celibate, reclusive life because they believe. It is probable that perhaps, ultimately, belief may lead one into such a life. I don't know. Various orders of belief, churches and trains of thought promote those things. Believers' paths could be different but that difference should not stand as a barrier to our belief in God.

Belief is a kind of intelligence that works from the inside and manifests itself in a way that others see (but not merely *for the purpose of* others seeing). Indeed, some manifestations may be dramatic, like the criminal who becomes a preacher, or the scrooge who becomes philanthropic. But if your life was not filled with extremes, the manifestation may be subtle. Who cares? The manifestation is not what leads to salvation.

Belief is a matter between you and God. God has a purpose for each of our lives and it is e̲ffected by our connection to God. Believing in him helps us to rely on his guidance in the things that we do. Whether those things are dramatic or subtle or vary from time to time is a matter of our connection and reliance on God's guidance of our lives. Whether you become a celibate preacher, reclusive monk, philanthropic tycoon or a soup kitchen volunteer is not for man to dictate.

We are each invited to partake in the bounty of shared gifts and live enriched lives. Engaging in prayer, we have resources to guide our lack, and to benefit from the munificence of God's bounty. Thinking and prayer are simultaneously resources and strengths. They are resources because we can use them whenever there is need. They are strengths because as part of us, they transform our lives and we improve in our abilities to cope.

"I believe" is a powerful declaration. It encircles unstated, implied elements. In its totality, it encompasses senses known and unknown; belief in one God; that the Bible is a Holy inspired record and guide; elements of trust; understanding of salvation. Many apostles of the Christian faith sum up their beliefs in the Apostles' Creed:

> *I believe in God, the Father Almighty,*
> *maker of heaven and earth;*
> *And in Jesus Christ his only Son, our Lord;*
> *who was conceived by the Holy Spirit,*
> *born of the Virgin Mary,*
> *suffered under Pontius Pilate,*
> *was crucified, died, and was buried;*
> *he descended into hell;*
> *the third day he rose from the dead;*
> *he ascended into heaven,*
> *and sits at the right hand of God the Father Almighty;*
> *from thence he shall come to judge the quick and the dead.*
> *I believe in the Holy Spirit,*
> *the holy universal church,*
> *the communion of saints,*
> *the forgiveness of sins,*
> *the resurrection of the body,*
> *and the life everlasting. Amen.*
>   See the United Methodist Church, www.umc.org

At the beginning of this chapter, we looked at Paul and Silas' call to believe and be saved. Believing in the Lord Jesus requires that we believe that Jesus was sent by God, and that his life on earth and his death bring salvation for us. The price of salvation has already been paid. Christ Jesus paid that price.

Wonderfully, it is open to all who believe, regardless of where you are right now. You don't first become good and then get saved.

By believing in God, we are strengthened and become a home in which the Spirit of God manifests its strength in this world. Overcoming hurdles to belief opens a life of faith through which good is revealed. That good manifests the presence of God.

Reflect and Explore:

A) Are there Christian beliefs that cause you doubt?

B) Reflect on the message in Revelation 19:10 and what this means for your perception of your relationship with others in your church and community.

C) Prayer [Based on Ephesians 2:12-22]: God of peace, bring me through the wall separating me from you. Let me no longer be a foreigner to you. Let me be part of one body united in Christ. Open my heart so that I am a fellow with all God's people united in his household. Let your spirit live within me.

Chapter 12: The Mystique of Christian Connectedness

Many different rituals, ceremonies and services are part of the customs and habits of Christian groups. Differences in worship -- including frequency, what is said, who may participate and other concerns -- can be distracting and sometimes foster feelings of disunity and suspicion both between Christian denominations and when viewed by non-Christians. However, these seemingly different churches form one connected family. Some Christian practices are observable by both Christians and non-Christians. Some ceremonies are quite spectacular. Less noticeable are Christian relationships and spiritual connectedness. I have selected perspectives of prayer, the mystifying communion of saints and the sometimes-complicated act of spiritual giving for our discussion.

A Rounded Perspective of Prayer

Prayer is often misunderstood. Prayer is sacred: communication with God both in words and in thought. The general perspective is that prayer is asking for something. Among popular prayers are requests for good health, healing, money and for forgiveness or help with whatever is of concern.

Less known are prayers of thanks, adoration and worship. To develop a rounded perspective of prayer, we must be familiar with the perspectives shared in Chapter 1 about eternal life, and the perspectives of the message Christ brought us through the many images discussed in Chapter 4. Guided by these understandings, the opportunity to pray is a way of maintaining an ongoing connection with God as we face the harsh realities of life.

The way we see God shapes our approach to prayer. Among the feelings shaping our attitudes to the professionals we approach for advice and help are: trust that they have the ability to help us, respect for them and deference to their counsel. We generally don't go to our doctors and lawyers demanding what we want. Similarly, when we approach God in prayer, we approach with reverence, trusting that he has the power to help, and even as we face unpleasant effects of life, knowing that our life and death are his counsel.

It is human to pray with passion, but it is a myth that our will and fervent prayer determine and define a favorable answer from God. When Christ was suffering, bearing the cross and making his way to be crucified, Christ asked God to take that experience, that cup, from him (Matthew 26:39). Yet, even though his humanity was wracked with distress, he showed trust in God's will. (Matthew 26:39 (ISV))

Later, during his crucifixion, wracked with excruciating pain, Christ called out in anguish, at about the ninth hour (three o'clock in the afternoon):

> ...*My God My God, why have you forsaken me?*
> *Matthew 25:46 ISV*

It is human to experience our ninth hour in some situation when we feel that all is lost. Christ's experience as described in those two passages is similar ours. We cry out, but even in our anguish we must trust God and his will for our lives.

Increasing the passion, adding bargains and making sacrifices and deals with God or paying for prayers are all inconsistent with the understanding that the answer to prayer is through God's grace. It is not that we must hide our anguish and pain. We approach God just as we are, *submitting to him*. Though our prayers may be fervent, submission, not fervency is the goal, (Hebrews 5:7). Relying on passion and sacrifices may lead to discouragement and disillusionment.

So then, how should we pray? There are many places in the Bible that provide guidance about prayer. These come together to form a rounded perspective to guide us through prayer. Prominent is The Lord's Prayer. In Matthew 6:9-13, Christ told the disciples:

> *In this manner, therefore, pray:*
> *Our Father in heaven,*

Hallowed be Your name.
Your kingdom come.
Your will be done
On earth as it is in heaven.
Give us this day our daily bread.
And forgive us our debts,
As we forgive our debtors.
And do not lead us into temptation,
But deliver us from the evil one.
For Yours is the kingdom and the power and the glory forever. Amen.
Matthew 6:9-13 NKJV

Recalling how Jesus taught his disciples is crucial to a prayerful approach to God. The Lord's Prayer begins by lifting God's name, his power and glory. It acknowledges God's holy supremacy (Matthew 6:9), and the prevailing reign of God's Kingdom and his will (Matthew 6:10). It also teaches us to bring our daily needs in prayer (Matthew 6:11) in the context of God's will (Matthew 6:10). In addition, the prayer teaches us to seek forgiveness, (Matthew 6:12) protection and deliverance (Matthew 6:13). Using this pattern, we also advocate for the state of God's kingdom, God's power and glory (Matthew 6:10 and 6:13, NKJV).

Awareness of this format in the Lord's Prayer may provide guidance and understanding as we pray. The manner is reverent and respectful, prayerfully seeking God's will on earth. We may not be in a state of calm when we begin to pray, but as faith is strengthened, we can let go of desperation and pray with confidence and trust, seeking only God's will.

Reverence isn't all that an attitude of prayer requires. Matthew 6:6 advises that we close the door and pray in private. Prayer is personal, private communication with God. Luke 5:16 also tells us that Jesus often went into the wilderness to pray, reinforcing this perspective. Much like taking a private phone call, in solitude and in quiet, we are better able to speak with God.

That is not to say that prayer in groups, congregations and in public gatherings is irreverent. Matthew 18 teaches us that sacred occasions arise when people come together in God's name. If a group is brought to a state of quiet reverence, and have assembled in God's name, prayer is appropriate. The call to pray in private is not in any way compromised by occasions where there is a leader in prayer and a reverent group in attendance. Sometimes we need to pray with others. The call against public showcase of prayer is more an admonishment for those who may purposely pray in public places, seeking admiration for their piousness.

Prayer may be likened more to ongoing communication than to sporadic submission of requests for help. 1 Thessalonians 5:17 urges us to pray continually. Many interpret this as a call to constantly repeat prayer requests. Yet, we are told in Matthew 6 not to utter vain repetitions in prayer. This may seem contradictory, but continual prayer is a call to ongoing, continual communication with God. Taken together with the charge to avoid repetitious prayer, we find further clarification that God hears our prayers and we must be connected to him continually through prayer. God hears us the first time we ask. The call to pray continually is encouragement to maintain that communion with God. Prayer is not only about requests for help.

In continual prayer God knows you. Prayer doesn't stop after you have asked for God's blessing. In contrast, with repetitious utterances we remain holding the burden, remembering and taking charge of it and keeping it in our possession. Maintaining a prayer list helps us keep the burden in our list of concerns. Instead, having put our burdens down, we give thanks and stay continually connected.

The Old Testament teaches that Daniel prayed three times a day at a time when he was concerned about a decree written by King Darius against prayer. The quick conclusion is that following Daniel's example, one should repeatedly demand a particular blessing. Instead, on closer reading, those prayers were prayers of thanks:

> *Three times a day he got down on his knees and prayed, giving thanks to his God, just as he had done before.*

Daniel 6:10 (NIV)

This promotes not repetition, but thankfulness. I have found that thankfulness not only helps me feel blessed even as I pray for new things, but also helps me count those assets, friends, talents, and other things that could be reassuring and helpful in the current situation. Gifts already received are a comfort to hold. As if calling in all the troops, their huge collective value is a reminder of God's goodness, an armor against feelings of defeat, and encouragement to be both humble and submissive to God. Acknowledging blessings can have a calming effect on the conversation of prayer. Thanksgiving is a comforting predisposition and a strong foundation for prayers.

Encouragement to offer thanksgiving is also one of the teachings in the passage we looked at in Thessalonians:

> *Rejoice always, pray continually, give thanks in all circumstances; for this is God's will for you in Christ Jesus.*
>
> *1 Thessalonians 5:16-18 (NIV)*

This passage aligns joy with thanksgiving and continual prayer and is often misconstrued as an invitation to make repetitive demands.

We can hardly discuss the distinction between continual prayer and repeated prayer without putting the popular story known as "The Persistent Widow" (Luke 18:1-8), in perspective.

Reading the account, we know that the judge is uncaring and selfish. In contrast, we know of God's kindness and benevolence. The judge granted her wish out of fear that she would continue to pester him. In contrast, God knows our needs before we even ask and grants them by his grace. Jesus often spoke in parables and there are patterns in each story that guide us to understand its hidden meaning. A parable is more than the surface story. Following the pattern, this repeated approach of the widow is therefore *in contrast* with our continual presence before God. We don't have to do what she did when faced with an uncaring judge. Instead, we come before a benevolent God who knows what we need even before we ask (Matthew 6:8).

A rounded perspective of prayer includes awareness of the things we pray for. Paul's letter to the Ephesians 6:18 urges us to pray for all kinds of needs and for all God's people. In that verse, Paul didn't stop at telling us to submit our requests in prayer:

> *... pray in the Spirit on all occasions with all kinds of prayers and requests. With this in mind, be alert and always keep on praying for all the Lord's people.*
>
> *Ephesians 6:18 (NIV)*

He urged not only that we pray in the Spirit, but also that we be alert and thirdly keep praying. When combined, they depict prayer as not merely a repetitive utterance of words, but engaging the alert self. We must be engaged in the process, enabling willing and deliberate communication with the divine through our spirit. "Keep on praying" echoes the call to continual prayer.

Skeptics may misinterpret prayer as a crutch for delusional people in a desperate situation. People of faith do not deny the reality of their circumstances, but understand that pain is typical of human life. In the context of the knowledge gained in this book, particularly chapters 1 and 4, faith in God's power is not constrained by harshness experienced in this world.

In some churches, one is invited to pay for prayers, including for those who have departed this life. The truth is that no amount of money could bribe God. Monies may legitimately go to support the cost of keeping a church open in today's realities, but no amount of money could determine a blessing from God, for persons dead or alive. It is through his grace and mercy not our sacrifices, that we receive. Return to chapter 6 for a more detailed discussion on common misconceptions about prayer.

Understandably, these may seem like contradictory and conflicting instructions. One may be called to ask what this says about how one should pray.

Two scriptures would sum up my answer to this question:

> *whatever you ask for in prayer, believe that you have received it, and it will be yours.*   Mark 11:24 (NIV)

and

> *your Father knows what you need before you ask him.* Matthew 6:8 (NIV)

In summary, we are encouraged to trust that God knows what we need before we ask, to pray without stopping, and to maintain communion with God, while not repeating thoughtless utterances. It is in that ongoing relationship that we submit to God, give thanks, ask and receive, seek and find.

An attitude of prayer includes different dimensions presented in texts of the Bible. The following illustration is included to provide guidance about these diverse dimensions. It is not intended to be a formula. Feel welcome to add your favorite verses to this chart.

An Attitude of Prayer

Biblical references are provided for reference and are not exhaustive

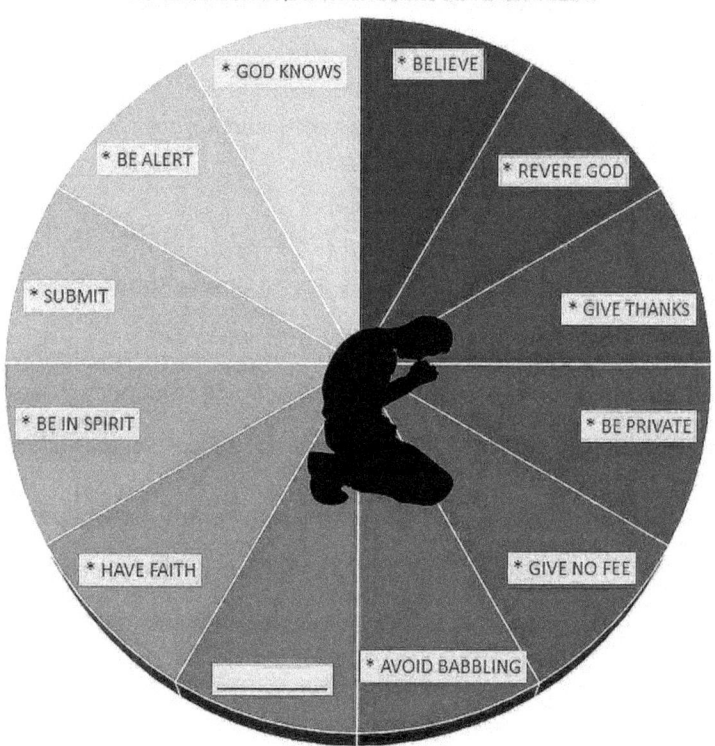

- Believe (Mark. 11:24)
- Be Thankful (Dan. 6)
- Prayer is free (Matt. 21:13, Rev. 22:17)
- Pray Continually (1 Thess. 5:16-18)
- Be in the Spirit (Eph. 6, 1 Cor. 14:15)
- Be Alert to needs of others (Eph 6:18)
- Be Reverent (Matt. 6:9)
- Pray in private (Matt 6:5-6)
- Avoid senseless repetition (Matt 6:7-8)
- Have Faith (James 1:6-7)
- Submit to God's Will (Matt. 6:10, 26:39)
- God knows what you need (Matt. 6:8)

Communion of Saints

Christians have hope that there is unity among God's believers: present and past. In this usage, the word "communion" evokes both the sacrament of Holy Communion, as well as the neutral concept of sharing, belonging and connecting conveyed by its Latin etymology communion- (commūniō) meaning "sharing" and (commūnis) meaning "common" (dictionary.com).

According to the etymology dictionary etymonline.com, the word "saint" was originally used as a prefix to the name of a canonized person, and later came to mean a "person of extraordinary holiness."

In this sense then, the communion of saints is the coming together, connection and sharing of all Christians. It conveys the sense that Christians are not separate, but united. It also captures the continuity of this relationship among Christians over history and connotes extraordinary power amplified by this connection.

Despite the lofty sounding term, the communion of saints is not an assembly to be worshipped and glorified, but more of a network to be embraced. The Bible teaches that even as part of the family of Christians, each of us has weaknesses (Romans 3:23), and as we saw in Revelation 19:10, an angel warns against worshipping even angels.

Through baptism, anyone who chooses may become part of the family of Christians. In practice, many churches establish gatekeepers who control who is permitted into fellowship. However, everyone is called to commit to a life connected to God through Christ. As in all cases, if a particular church closes its doors to you, forgive them and move on. God wants you to come to him.

The communion of saints is not merely religious dogma, but a living aspect of Christianity. As a Christian, one enters into this communion, bringing one's gifts and talents into service for the common good (1 Corinthians 12:7). In connecting with each other and with saints, we are equal, each with different skills, talents and roles to play (1 Corinthians 12:12-14). That communion brings together elements of the Body of Christ, manifesting Christ's divine power through a network of disparately gifted people.

The expression "the Body of Christ" refers to the unity of people who by being Christian, represent and give life to Christ's mission and life on earth. Christians as a body continue Christ's teaching, broadcast his message to each new generation and repeat the story of his life.

Although different churches today have different rules governing membership and appoint administrative and religious heads, they have no say in anyone's membership in the communion of saints and the body of Christ. No decree can effectively exclude anyone or grant anyone a higher status than another in the communion of saints. It may operate on earth but it is not of earthly origin. Instead, the Bible teaches that:

> *God has placed the parts in the body, every one of them, just as he wanted them to be...*
>
> *God has put the body together, giving greater honor to the parts that lacked it, so that there should be no division in the body, but that its parts should have equal concern for each other. If one part suffers, every part suffers with it; if one part is honored, every part rejoices with it.*
>
> *Now you are the body of Christ, and each one of you is a part of it.*
>
> *1 Corinthians 12:18 and 24-27 (NIV)*

Churches do their best to preserve belief in Christ and adopt many different approaches to administering and managing the complex organizations throughout the world. Administrative and financial roles may be associated with having kept the church alive over centuries of change, and are respected. But the church serves a greater purpose than its buildings and its administrative and financial pursuits. All church law and practices must hang on two primary commandments: to love God and to love our neighbor as ourselves, (Matthew 22:40). As the complexity of organizations increases, churches may need to recalibrate their practices to honor Christ's mission and purpose.

Giving from the Spirit

The church is just not another business trying to get your money or another charity begging you for help. Opportunities for nurturing Christian values include giving to the poor, feeding the hungry, and providing comfort, shelter, healing and other kinds of support as appropriate to those in need. Similar to social services, these are all good Christian pursuits. They are different in that Christian acts of kindness have two dimensions: the visible act of service to the person in need and the participation of the Christ-loving spirit. On their own, without embracing the spiritual dimension, these acts are social services, equivalent to those conducted by governments, merchants, or businesses seeking tax write-offs or other goals. First Corinthians 13 expresses it this way:

> *And though I bestow all my goods to feed the poor, and though I give my body to be burned, but have not love, it profits me nothing.*
>
> *1 Corinthians 13:3 (NKJV)*

This verse drives home the primacy of love over all the acts of kindness that are part of Christian service. Christian service is not merely about giving food, comfort, making donations to charities and other ways in which we help the less fortunate. Those are indeed good services. Yet this verse emphasizes that Christian service is about love, the participation of the loving spirit in service. Even though we may perform the most notable acts of service, donate millions to a group cause, and make the most extreme sacrifices, if the acts are performed without love, it is not the service required of the Christian spirit.

Several years ago, there was a disastrous storm in New Jersey and many homes were destroyed in one night of hurricane winds and rain. Homes along the shore were wrecked by unprecedented surges of ocean waves, rain and winds or swept away in violent currents or the aftermath of weakened foundations, shattered structures and receding tides. Towns, roads and community infrastructure were destroyed by Hurricane Sandy and remained shaken for years during the struggle to rebuild. Christian groups sprung up to help these communities and created many opportunities for hands-on service and giving. Some people wrote checks and donated generously to purchase material, while others rolled up their sleeves and got to work shoulder to shoulder in acts of kindness, rebuilding destroyed homes and giving generously to those whose homes were casualties of the natural disaster. Many people were touched by the disastrous experience and felt joy in helping to restore the losses of the needy.

In addition to these hands-on opportunities for service, many churches provide other opportunities for members to participate in ongoing acts of giving and service. People make commitments to give and dutifully support the work of the church.

Whether it is joining a church-sponsored project to help rebuild a community, responding to a church's call to help someone facing disaster or contributing financially to a church project, participation is not an automatic ticket to salvation. The acts themselves, even giving one's body to be burned or other extreme sacrifices, if performed without the commitment of the spirit, the love, the participation of the heart-- even those acts are not what the foundation of Christian faith demands. Referring again to 1 Corinthians 13:3, *even if you give your body to be burned,* and you do not simultaneously have love, there is no Christian grace in the act.

The point is, we cannot bribe God with our performances. God sees our hearts and knows whether we write that check to get some tax write-off and whether we join the community rebuilding project because we are lonely, just want to keep busy or are seeking to enjoy a fun experience with friends. Nothing is *wrong* with those desires. They are good and healthy ways of coping with life. If one does them enough, they teach us to make wholesome choices and live clean lives.

Public acts of giving are the fabric of impressive obituaries, biographies and admired life stories. They set a grand spectacle, perhaps also inspire others and leave sparkling footprints in the annals of our recorded lives. But the foundation of Christian belief requires that every act be done with love.

Public figures may boast about the wonderful things they have done and allot huge chunks of wealth they allot to support charitable efforts. That is very welcome. Yet, Christ-like giving is not boastful and isn't pursued for fame and accolades. When Christians boast and seek praise, reasoning people recognize givers' personal goals and may become skeptical about goals of Christian giving. There may be reasons why pastors and congregations brag about their donations and good deeds, and they do receive the expected reward. That is not the path to take. Christian giving is humble:

> *When you give to the needy, do not announce it with trumpets, as the hypocrites do in the synagogues and on the streets, to be honored by others. Truly I tell you, they have received their reward in full. But when you give to the needy, do not let your left hand know what your right hand is doing, so that your giving may be in secret.*
>
> *Matthew 6:2-4 (NIV)*

Money itself does not change people and communities. The Christian belief is that love, patience and kindness are the bases for transformation. The Bible sums it up this way:

> *If I give all I possess to the poor and give over my body to hardship that I may boast, but do not have love, I gain nothing. Love is patient, love is kind. It does not envy, it does not boast, it is not proud. It does not dishonor others, it is not self-seeking, it is not easily angered, it keeps no record of wrongs. Love does not delight in evil but rejoices with the truth. It always protects, always trusts, always hopes, always perseveres.*
>
> 1 Corinthians 13:3-7 (NIV)

Giving of one's wealth is good, but giving of one's heart is what distinguishes Christ-like giving.

Donations are welcome and often inspiring. Donors must be thanked for their contributions. It is a good social principle that those with excess give to those with fewer possessions. Society needs that and there is nothing wrong that it also profits donors. However, there is more to our lives than the physical acts of giving. While wealth is valuable, Christian service is more rewarding.

In the chapter on abundant life, we discussed Christ's explanation of the difficulty in separating acts of giving from acts of Christian service:

> *And again I say to you, it is easier for a camel to go through the eye of a needle than for a rich man to enter the kingdom of God.*
>
> Matthew 19:24 (NKJV)

At the heart of this statement is the principle that one can act from earthly wealth or from the wealth of spiritual delight. There is nothing *wrong* with wealth, but there is more to Christian goodness and charity than material wealth. Even though we do prosper on earth, Christian goodness and charity are independent of physical wealth. Our prosperity is bestowed through God's benevolence toward us.

The verse above highlights the dichotomy between spiritual and physical wealth. Physical wealth can make one oblivious to the fountain of spiritual wealth, so much so that a rich man can have as much trouble acting from spiritual wealth as a camel would have attempting to squeeze its huge physical body through the small eye of a needle.

Giving from the spirit is not about how much or how major the project or how dramatic the sacrifice. Many churches include their biggest donors in their administrative bodies, publicly acknowledge the *amount* that people contribute and establish systems that encourage more giving, competitive contributions and larger and larger donations. It is understood that the church needs money to maintain and support its mission and property.

The dilemma is that while the physical *means* of the church may demand funding and depend on acts of giving no matter the source of wealth, the spiritual *purpose* of the church demands giving at the urge of our spiritual wealth. The demands of economic survival may have a different compass from the spiritual purpose of spiritual survival. Not surprisingly, it is also one of the bases for the convictions of skeptics that the church is merely another money-making machine.

There is no question that there are real concerns that challenge the survival of the Christian church. In today's world, maintaining the tangible assets, communications, outreach and structure of the church requires participation in the economy. In the 2013 movie, *The Wolf of Wall Street*, the lead character, a millionaire Wall Street stock broker and immoral wolf whose compass was money, described a benefit of wealth as the help it can provide to churches financially. While money may be necessary to maintain the physical church, it is important that churches not become *The Wolf on Church Street* with a similar financial compass. The compass of spiritual purpose is superior to monetary wealth, and the value it adds to the human condition is fundamental. Yes, money may add value, but is a tenuous component of human life and an unsteady compass.

A church's relationship with money can affect its ability to reach out to the spirit of thinking people. They see through money making ventures and know all the tricks in the book. The church will likely gain funds as shrewd investors seek tax write-offs for contributions to registered charities, but lose souls if it is considered merely another a financial investment. It is for the church to determine which is more important. People seeking God should recognize this and not be daunted by the way some churches operate.

Renowned economist Adam Smith's sixteenth century groundbreaking and well-respected work *An Inquiry into the Nature and Causes of The Wealth of Nations* can help us understand the reality of money. Smith concluded that the exchangeable value of any possession is directly related to the power it gives the person who tenders it. In other words, we pay money for things that have for us the same value power as the money we are paying. For example, if it is raining excessively and pure water is collecting everywhere, no one is going to pay for water. But in a severe drought when there is no water anywhere, people would be inclined to give just about anything in exchange for it. In that case, your willingness to pay for water would be in direct proportion to how severely your life depended on it.

The Bible presents a similar perspective. In the story of the widow's mite (Luke 21:1-4), it defines the poor widow's willingness to contribute from her scarce resources as in fact of greater value than contributions made from those who possessed abundance:

> *...this poor widow has put in more than all; for all these out of their abundance have put in offerings for God, but she out of her poverty put in the entire livelihood that she had."*
>
> Luke 21:3-4 NKJV

To the widow, the value she saw in giving to God was worth every penny: all the livelihood she owned. In contrast, the wealthy give to God only a (meagre) portion of their wealth, even though the actual amount may have been more than the amount of the widow's gifts. The residuals given by a wealthy tycoon are not sums that he needs. He may even profit in the form of tax rebates from such giving. Unlike the widow, he is not giving his all: his everything. His contribution is based on a principle of economics and assessments of what is good enough.

This illustrates how spiritual purpose is supreme over monetary wealth. While the amount of money may be a factor in the life of the church, the whole commitment and total selfless giving is closer to what is demanded of the Christian heart. Hence, the poor widow, by giving despite poverty, offered more than all who gave from abundance.

This perspective teaches that we cannot bribe God by the amount we give. Certainly, we may impress the church accountants, financial bean counters and even the heads of our churches who may look into how much is given and make challenging appeals for giving. We can write checks, donate and dole out as abundantly as we dare. We can also share out of guilt or a sense of duty. That giving helps the church and all the worthy purposes of charity. Feeding the hungry, shelter for the poor and destitute, clothing for those in need: these are the valued products of the vibrant church in the world. Whatever is given to a worthy cause is a welcome gift for others. From any perspective, the purpose and goal of giving are good and worthy.

I suspect that churches that neglect their spiritual purpose will eventually fail as churches. The essential teaching in the parable of the widow's mite is the importance of the heart of the giver, not the gift or donation alone. That may not be important to operation of a business concern, but a church that attempts the business route is a weak competitor in that universal arena where people weigh and choose what they want to spend money on.

A carefully measured ten percent from the wealthy will definitely surpass the amount of giving from a carefully measured ten percent of the less affluent, yet both have the same source of the caring spirit. Similarly, the generously donated tax margin savings are astute donations to the worthy quest of the church.   It is good to be astute and to smartly manage the financial and other gifts and blessings one receives.

It is also good to give to the church, support worthy causes, and contribute offerings for the poor. Giving is good: just know that there is more to be done in the search for God.

What God wants is the whole heart. God cares about the *source* of the giving-- your heart and soul. Though some may count and measure the amount of a gift, and possibly translate that amount into a meaning about the heart of the gift, it isn't necessarily correct. The Bible urges us not to perform spiritual acts for the benefit of others. If we are seeking reward from God, it is the heart behind the giving that counts:

> *Be careful not to practice your righteousness in front of others to be seen by them. If you do, you will have no reward from your Father in heaven.*
> *Matthew 6:1 (NIV)*

Nothing is inherently *wrong* with giving to impress others. It is not illegal, but it is not the route for spiritual giving. One may see that it has a place in social or political advancement and acceptance in some circles, and can probably be justified for various socially acceptable reasons. I am not condemning anyone's action and the participation of members of the Christian church in any kind of social activity. Social activity is a different dimension. In all giving, we must understand what we are doing and not mistake all our ritual acts of giving for Christ like giving. Some people remain skeptical because of systems of ritual giving that exhibit the church as a financial venture.

What could be clearer than Matthew 6:1-4? Tactics such as maintaining public lists of donors, donations and contributions, parading donors through the aisles of churches position public reward against public embarrassment. Proceeds may very well go to support worthy causes and can no doubt be justified. True, there is that reward. Who doesn't want to be associated with a grand cause and be praised and admired by the congregation and the world? Who doesn't want to avoid the disdain of fellow members and citizens? Social giving has its place and perhaps that place can be justified in particular situations.

Spiritual giving according to the principles taught by Christ is without public fanfare. It is not for me or anyone to tell us that our giving makes us Christian. It is through the grace of God that our giving is rewarded. God sees our hearts and I would be presumptuous to say that he doesn't want us to be embarrassed in a congregation that parades giving for public scrutiny. Each of us has the opportunity for public and secret charitable deeds. There are all kinds of contexts of giving. We each face some kind of encouragement or temptation. While we do need to function in a community, at the same time, each of us has the opportunity to choose to render our hearts in full to God.

Reflect and Explore:

A) Share ideas about prayers that don't ask for something

B) Write down a few things you could say to someone who shares with you that they have been given news about a terminal illness

C) Reflect on the chart illustrating an attitude of prayer and any ways that this helps you in prayer.

D) Read Revelation 19:9-10 and reflect on what this means for your group of worshippers.

E) Reflect with others (leaders and members together) on Romans 3:22-24 and what this means for your role together.

Chapter 13: Jokes and Taunts that Go "Boom" in the Light

In addition to inclusive and exclusive rituals, I have observed a few things that seem to make some people uncomfortable about Christian beliefs:

- some beliefs cannot be verified
- some aspects of faith defy scientific laws
- people cite scientific conclusions to disprove elements of faith
- some people may laugh at and ridicule people and their faith
- some answers to prayers are disappointing
- some leaders in the Christian churches commit crimes and misdemeanors and show themselves untrustworthy
- different faith groups describe and practice faith differently
- the Bible documents dishonest activities by Christians
- faith groups fight each other
- members of the same congregation sometimes have antagonistic relationships

- leaders in churches sometimes break commandments
- the church is filled with "hypocrites" who go to church one day and sin for six
- enslavement of black people persisted for four hundred years
- racial inequalities prevail in many forms throughout the world
- unjust social systems flourish
- unjust legal decisions and systems often triumph over justice
- exclusionary political systems dominate even Christian societies
- people die even when prayed for or don't get what they pray for
- unfair and tragic things happen even to those who profess faith

People ask: Where is God? How could there be a good and powerful God when there is so much wrong? Some conclude that there is no God. Some people dismiss Christianity as fiction because they seek tangible scientific evidence that no one could provide, or because they can point to occurrences that they interpret as evidence that God could not possibly exist. Some are simply embarrassed because people who teach and whom they trust present theories and explain science as if theories were conclusive, indisputable fact. Evolution is one such theory that many teachers uphold as if it were fact.

From our legal systems, we learn to trust contemporary tangible physical evidence. The fact that we do not have photographs of Christ and his disciples, Moses and the Jews, a video of Noah and the great flood, Adam, Eve and the stories of faith fuel questions of disbelief and are unsettling to those whose minds have been disciplined and educated in contemporary methods.

That same education encourages a comfort level with incompleteness of theories presented by people singled out for respect. We are comfortable with theories of evolution even though there are missing links, accept conclusions based on examination of fossils even though those findings make assumptions and the proponents themselves advise caution. There are many who read only approved texts and look to particular sources to suggest reading material. The final effect is that our perspectives are shaped and defined by an established system of learning. It is difficult for many people to think for themselves and uncomfortable for them to hold thoughts and beliefs unless they are introduced through the education system.

Understandably, we can share what we touch, see and hear, and capture them to share with each other even after they have passed. Photographs, audio and video recordings help us capture those realities. We also interpret them through forms of art, drawing and writing, and those who dare try to share the realities of their spiritual existence using the same tools.

Since the mid twentieth century, Christianity has not been taught in US public schools. It is therefore understandable why we may feel embarrassed about faith and belief and feel pressured to adopt popular positions of disbelief. It is simply not part of the shared education. That education is acquired outside of the school system, separating faith from state and damaging the perception of faith and belief in God as upstanding and credible.

With this in mind, it is understandable that taunts can shake people's faith and fear of taunts can keep some away from churches. Any single factor that cannot be verified can serve, in some people's minds, to discredit the whole. Any misbehaving cleric confirms for them the absence of truth in the whole system; any aspect of faith that defies science loses its ground to disbelief; scientific conclusions are upheld to disprove elements of faith; the prospect of laughter and ridicule serve to scare people away from disclosing their faith and may encourage disbelief. There are even pastors who deny some accounts in the Bible in deference to scientific *beliefs* and argue that the church that upholds particular Christian beliefs prevents non-Christians from accepting Christianity.

Foundations of faith explode if prayers aren't followed by the outcome people ask for or someone dies even after fervent prayer to save their lives. More so, when history shows years of suffering for people of faith including social injustices, racial inequalities and unfair social and political systems that flourish even in Christian societies. People point to over four hundred years of slavery and ask "where is God in that?" It doesn't help when different Christian groups describe and practice rituals of faith differently, faith groups fight each other, or members of the same congregation display antagonistic relationships. In addition, non-believers can cite within the Bible accounts of dishonesty and lack of faith and can pick one story or another in a kind of "gotcha" concerning proof that God's people are no better than others.

Indeed, unfair and tragic things occur even in the lives of those who profess trust in God. I began this book with the assertion that we're all going to die. So too, belief in God does not exempt us from the trials and challenges of life. The Christian faith welcomes all and Christ's salvation is open even to sinners. Sadly, leaders in Christian churches sometimes do commit crimes, misdemeanors or untrustworthy acts. I make no excuse for them because their role is to lead and set the Christian example. However, we must understand that although some set themselves apart as if they are themselves God, they are not.

We are all human. We are all on a journey. We each start as unlearned babies, without speech or language and we learn to speak from those around us, learn the vocabulary of the world and learn to read as we are taught. We may even be smarter than our parents whose language we adopt. We may even learn more than they and go further in our education than they did. So too, our faith is not circumscribed by those who teach. I have been able to learn about God and become stronger in my faith, *despite* evident weaknesses in teachers. No one's mistake is reason for any of us to become disenchanted with God. No one's shortcomings are satisfactory reasons to keep us from our quest to find God.

In his book "Eternal Life: A New Vision," (HarperOne, NY, 2009) Rev. John Shelby Spong, retired Anglican Bishop, wrote about his disillusionment after a lifetime in the Church. The compassion I felt as I read of his disillusionment fueled my determination to write this book. What other people say does affect our faith. It is human to look to each other for approval. If we are laughed at, mocked, or are seen as different from our peers, we might step back unless we had strong conviction and understanding.

It is true that some go to church one day a week and spend the rest of the week ignoring Christian values. The challenge for searching Christians is to love those people and recognize their journey, but not let it keep them from fellowship with God. It is important to remember that everyone is on a journey. Going to church does not mean that a person has completed the journey. Learn from your experiences and keep out of the fray on your journey. There are other things to learn and grow through fellowship with others. Your gifts may strengthen others, but you need compassion and strength to use them when you see the need. Labeling others as hypocrites may be comforting justification for isolating one's self. However, we also keep our gifts out of the pool.

Let me share with you the true story of Kathy Noms (not her real name). Kathy became frustrated with a particular pastor at her church. The whole experience of Sunday worship was disappointing to her. She was restless and felt empty at the end of Sunday services. Kathy decided to move on and try other churches. She visited a church where she felt very welcome and received an enlightening and filling message. Among friendly people serving unselfishly under the guidance of a strong pastor, Kathy felt the spirit of God alive in that church. But as she basked in the warmth at that church, she felt compassion for her friends at her old church. Instead of joining the new, friendly congregation, Kathy felt inspired to go back to her old church and start a separate program outside the Sunday service. The disappointing pastor became involved in the program and, according to Kathy, seemed to come alive, showing pastoral skills that were not evident in the Sunday service. Kathy also grew, as did the program. It served to enrich the mission of the church.

Sometimes, crossing a hurdle of discomfort can propel you further on the journey to find God. Ignoring it or isolating oneself can stifle gifts and blessings yet undiscovered. What may seem like an obstacle keeping you from God may be a hurdle to cross to reveal the God you seek. Remember that our education system has no programs for spiritual education. Uncomfortable situations, discomfiting jokes and taunts are seeds of discomfort: often the only clues to tell you that you've had enough at one level. It is the clue that you need to guide you in your quest to grow spiritually.

We need strong conviction to withstand the pressures to live up to the expectations of our peers and live down their prejudices and taunts. Frivolous taunts such as whether Jesus was born on December 25, whether he was killed by the Jews, whether Moses was Egyptian or Levite, Israelite, of Jewish faith etc., are not the critical issues fundamental to a relationship with God. It takes persistence to keep seeking beyond the minutiae of details to find the truth about God.

We may doubt our human capacity to understand truths beyond intangibles, yet it is accepted that we use only a small portion of our brain. The result is that our ability to reach beyond formal teachings and contemporary practices is not fully developed. I am going to relate a story of extreme human capacity. Research by Harvard Professor Herbert Benson (Benson, Herbert, M.D. and Proctor, William, Your Maximum Mind, Random House of Canada, Inc. Toronto, 1987), explored the capabilities of human beings. Benson observed Tibetan monks control their body temperatures such that they were able to stay outdoors through a light snowfall during subzero temperatures. In contrast, our education system does not teach us to perform such feats. We are educated to use only particular aspects of our brain capacities. Among other capacities that our education neglects or limits is the development of our instinct for truth. We are discouraged from belief in spiritual realities in preference for the realities defined by our sight, touch and hearing.

While the case of the Tibetan monks' survival in the snowstorm may be exceptional, and we think of them as virtually a different kind of human, somehow unlike ourselves, we may, regardless of what we are taught, begin to perceive extended capacities in ourselves as we hear of ordinary people like ourselves who perform exceptionally. Our minds are only partly educated. In the formal systems of education, our spirits are hardly educated at all.

Reflect and Explore:

A) Review the list at the beginning of this chapter. Are there items in this list that you have experienced or heard expressed by others?

B) Discuss other experiences not in this list that you can add to identify concerns that impede expressions of faith and deter Christians.

C) What kinds of help, either in this chapter, in other parts of the book or elsewhere, do you believe could be used to overcome deterrents to Christian faith?

D) Consider the impact of your formal education in your life of faith.

Chapter 14: Things Hoped For

The Bible defines faith as the substance of things hoped for and the evidence of things not seen (Hebrews 11:1, KJV). Although the Bible records many extraordinary accounts, we must distinguish them from those that are still to be seen. Christians recognize that things hoped for cannot be perceived with our five senses. They are indeed extraordinary. In the same way that the mere idea of cyber friends would have been scoffed at when Charles Babbage designed the first computer in 1952, or the idea of Big Brother seemed so fictionalized as recently as 1949 when George Orwell wrote the book 1984, the *status quo* does not invalidate an extraordinary hope. Instead, things hoped for are the light of what remains to be seen.

The Resurrection of the Body

Christians believe that Christ lived, died and was resurrected. People subsequently spoke and ate with him, touched the wounds of his crucifixion and left a message that we too may know. It is recognized as an extraordinary occurrence that lights the hope Christians have of their own resurrection, largely based on the mystifying label "firstfruits" attached to it (1 Corinthians 15:20-23). Given the limits of our human experience of life and death, resurrection of the human body is not fully understood. These same limits of perception lead many to debate Christ's resurrection. Like caterpillars gripping onto tangible branches, we can hardly perceive that aspect of our nature that could spawn a butterfly. Christians acknowledge these limitations and accord resurrection of the body the prestige of hope.

Life Everlasting

Earlier in this book, we addressed the concept of eternal life. It is one of the gifts hoped for. It is a gift of faith. Christians believe that at baptism, one is granted membership into the family of Christ, with access to the promise of eternal life. Baptizing babies who cannot choose for themselves is done with the hope that the act of baptism dedicates the life of the baby to God. A child that may not live to the age of reason is through his parents' faith offered up to receive the gift of eternal life from God. Christians are not sure exactly what everlasting living will be like. Review of the clues to the kingdom of heaven discussed earlier in this book, paint pictures using analogies familiar to this world. Despite all the clues and interpretations, it is still to be seen.

Paradise

Paradise is another hoped-for prize. While on the cross, Christ spoke of paradise (Luke 23:43) to one of the accused on a cross beside him, promising to meet the man there. Christians hope that the paradise of God is a blissful experience where they will be nourished by the source of life. (Rev. 2:7) The expectation of inexpressible abundance, joy and spectacle stemming from the report in 2 Cor. 12:4 is the substance of things hoped for in this paradise. Inexpressible "things" cannot be put into words, much less proven. The expectation that those things are good, not harmful, is faith.

Our understanding of "victorious" in the promise in Rev. 2:7 leads Christians to expect something inexpressibly good. Yet, the fact that Christ expected to meet the criminal in paradise is baffling to our sense of victory as the opposite of defeat; of winning as the opposite of losing; of criminal as the opposite of Christ. We are left to puzzle over these understandings in the context of the promise. If the criminal could experience paradise with our Savior, what does this mean for our quest to experience it? Connected with eternal life is the hope that that life will be in communion with Christ and with indescribable good provisions for us.

Era of Purpose

Humans also hope that this life is an era of purpose. We can hardly perceive the 'big picture' of which our lives are but a pixel. The Bible promises that there is a purpose of glory springing from this humble life:

> [Our Savior] will transform our lowly bodies so that they will be like his glorious body.
>
> Philippians 3:21 (NIV)

First Peter refers to the idea of rebirth into life again. Specifically:

> Praise be to the God and Father of our Lord Jesus Christ! In his great mercy, he has given us new birth into a living hope through the resurrection of Jesus Christ from the dead.
>
> 1 Peter 1:3 (NIV)

Some people find it difficult to understand their lot in this life, much less to appreciate a bigger context in which their life matters. In that sense, the premise that this is an era of purpose is one of the things hoped for. People hope that living on earth has meaning and purpose. In that hope, the pursuit of life becomes a question of how to live. The Bible recommends:

> now you are light in the Lord. Live as children of light (for the fruit of the light consists in all goodness, righteousness and truth) and find out what pleases the

Lord. Have nothing to do with the fruitless deeds of darkness, but rather expose them.

Ephesians 5:8-11 (NIV)

The Bible offers an embedded lesson plan to make life into an era of purpose. Purpose is therefore both something hoped for and something we can act on. Hebrews 12 defines life as a race and proposes that we use Jesus' life as a pattern, keeping our eyes on his life, and regarding any hardships we encounter as discipline from God. This imagery is consistent with the assessment of life as a journey with a destination that is a prize at the end of a path properly travelled. It fuels hope that ours has purpose.

In God's Hands

The hope that this is an era of purpose means that we must successfully cross all the hurdles and overcome all the obstacles on the path of living life as children of light. If the obstacles and hardships are discipline from God, it means that they are situations to respond to, leaving our lives in God's hands. Like an obstacle course, tough situations must be overcome before the prize is won. Self-destruction means that we drop out of the race before it is over. How could one get the prize if the end is not reached?

As a general rule, anyone who feels discouraged can find refuge in God. People also need each other through this journey. Christians believe that God's grace is attainable by ordinary, simple people. They form a network and churches to provide support and direction so anyone can receive God's grace. In reality, some churches stop particular people from sharing in this network and may close their doors and deny misfits and one kind of sinner or another the opportunity to gain the support of Christian brothers and sisters and the guidance and instruction of teachers. Fortunately, some other churches welcome everyone seeking God, recognizing that everyone falls short and that those in need include sinners. No one should be discouraged by how particular people, however well robed, choose to operate particular houses of worship.

Unlike many gallant examples in the Bible-- Moses, Noah and the prophets who seem born to greatness -- Job's suffering makes him more of an example for us to believe that God's grace is attainable by ordinary, wounded, sad and alienated people with misfortunes just like ours. Job's ultimate reward after he had suffered the most grievous challenges brings hope to people who may feel that suicide is an option:

> *The Lord blessed the latter part of Job's life more than the former part.*
>
> *Job 42:12 (NIV)*

We are faced with many options as we live from day to day. We actively participate in those options. When each day looks just like the last, life can seem interminable and the effort to face another day of similar hardship may appear futile. The Bible helps Christians put such experiences in perspective. It is not that Christians do not experience similar incidents. Instead, simply knowing that that is common helps Christians deal with it. Knowing what is to come gives Christians fortitude to face pitfalls characteristic of life. Imagine the confusion if a mother did not know that she was pregnant until the baby arrived! In the same way that an expectant mother is prepared for the life-changing experience of childbirth, we prepare and learn through the Bible from those who have gone before. In God's hands, whether we live or die, we can face life's trials with our eyes fixed on our purpose.

> *I only know that in every city the Holy Spirit warns me that prison and hardships are facing me. However, I consider my life worth nothing to me; my only aim is to finish the race and complete the task the Lord Jesus has given me*
>
> *Acts 20:23-24 (NIV)*

Hope of Love

People experience love and can do little to describe it. It is a powerful, all-consuming experience, an inexplicable miracle. For some, it is the *only* experience that makes life on earth bearable. Christians believe that God loves them and are taught that God's love transcends the powerful experience of our human love. That inexplicable, all-encompassing experience connects us to others and to God. It sends us searching again and again to repeat the experience. Love gives us hope and helps us persist in life.

Those of us who have had the good fortune to have experienced love know we can't describe it adequately in words. Although the experience of love can hardly be proven with standards of legal evidence, it drives and sustains people's lives. Through love, even people who challenge Christian beliefs for lack of evidence are invited to the hope of inexplicable things experienced without explicit evidence. Love is the bedrock of God's immortal, invisible provisions.

Forgiveness- The Promise

Christians believe that there is right and wrong and that God has the power to forgive the wrongs that we do. Forgiveness is the act of removing the burden that results from wrong. Unless one has experienced that burden, one can hardly understand forgiveness. Wrongdoing affects both the perpetrator and the victim. Forgiveness from the victim can bring relief to both. It is also true that forgiveness of the perpetuator (forgiveness of self) may not ease the victim's suffering.

The word "forgive" has origins in Old Testament translation of the Hebrew word "nasa" which, according to InternetBibleCollege.com, means to take away guilt, iniquity or transgression. We are taught in The Lord's Prayer to ask God to forgive our debts or trespasses *as we forgive our debtors*, linking our request for God to forgive us to our own forgiveness of others. That tells us that God applies the same justice to us as we apply to others. Herein lies our hope. Forgiveness from God is a prayer, and one of the things hoped for is that God will grant that forgiveness.

The parable about the king whose servant was punished for all he owed because the servant did not forgive his fellow servants of their debt to him (Matthew 18:21-35) links our forgiveness of others to our forgiveness from God. It may be noted that the servant's forgiveness was *revoked* because of his inability to later forgive. It is testament that the hope of forgiveness is not a single act, pertaining to a single incident. Failure to forgive today may result in revocation of previously forgiven misdeeds.

> *"This is how my heavenly Father will treat each of you unless you forgive your brother or sister from your heart."*
>
> *Matthew 18:35 (NIV)*

In practice, forgiveness may require understanding of the perpetrator and compassion for them. We cannot merely *say* that we forgive. Christian forgiveness must be more than a speech. To venture on a path to continuously forgive may require understanding that, like those who harm us, we also have weaknesses and may also do wrong. Although one may not commit an equally grievous hurt, acknowledging our own flaws and imperfections may help us to genuinely forgive anyone of the most heinous acts.

The Second Coming

For the message of his second coming, we rely on Jesus' teaching to his disciples before he died. He said:

> *You heard me say, 'I am going away and I am coming back to you.*

> John 14:28, NIV

The promise of another coming of Jesus is also found in Acts 1:11. Witnesses to his departure from earth were told, by two unnamed men dressed in white:

> *This same Jesus, who has been taken from you into heaven, will come back in the same way you have seen him go into heaven*

> Acts 1:11, NIV

The expectation then is that Jesus will come again in "the same way" that he was seen to leave. Other translations use the expression "in like manner." Whether this means the manner of ascent will be the same manner or the vision of Jesus will be the same is moot. The essential message is that Jesus will return. Whatever the "same way' or "like manner," what is important is that we recognize the event and not be perplexed by occurrences that we are persuaded are indicative of it. It is also recorded in Matthew 24:30 that Jesus told his disciples that the sign of his second coming will appear "in heaven." We must know for ourselves and be sure.

The second coming of the Savior has not yet occurred. We are warned in Matthew 24:27 that we will have no doubt when the Savior returns to earth again:

> *For as lightning that comes from the east is visible even in the west, so will be the coming of the Son of Man.*
>
> *Matthew 24:27 (NIV)*

The Bible also warns that there will be imposters declaring that they are the expected salvation. These verses in Matthew suggest that if we have any doubt, then it has not yet occurred. One can therefore completely ignore anyone who declares that they are the expected Christ. That event is not going to be revealed in a speech. The second coming will be an event that will be evident across the nations in the same way that lightning is visible from east to west.

The second coming is one of the hoped-for Christian occurrences. The expectation of a second coming is based on Jesus' promise to his disciples that he would come again:

> *you also must be ready, because the Son of Man will come at an hour when you do not expect him.*
> *Matthew 24:44 (NIV)*

It is also referred to in other scriptures. 2 Timothy 4:1 leads us to expect that both the living and the dead will be subject to judgment. Therefore, if you are alive when the time of judgment arrives, you will receive that judgment. It remains unclear whether the judgment of the dead occurs at the time that they die, or at a singular judgment day. The parable of the wise and foolish maidens who both fall asleep, then awake to meet the bridegroom suggests a period of sleeping before the second coming. This is consistent with a later judgment.

The hope is that there is some relief to come for both the living and the dead at the second coming. Many Christian denominations subscribe to this hope in the Apostles Creed. The creed voices the expectation that after he was resurrected, Christ ascended into heaven, and that he sits at the right hand of God, from where he shall come to judge the quick and the dead.

World Without End

The Bible leads us to expect that the world will not come to an end (Ephesians 3:21, Ecclesiastes 1:4). However political, geographic, ecological and other systems as we know them will not stand still. (Matthew 24:6-8)

We are also presented with discussion of "the end" (Matthew 22:14). However, the message is cryptic, requiring interpretation:

> *this gospel of the kingdom will be preached in the whole world as a testimony to all nations, and then the end will come.*
>
> *"So when you see standing in the holy place 'the abomination that causes desolation,' spoken of through the prophet Daniel—let the reader understand— then let those who are in Judea flee to the mountains. Let no one on the housetop go down to take anything out of the house. Let no one in the field go back to get their cloak. How dreadful it will be in those days for pregnant women and nursing mothers! Pray that your flight will not take place in winter or on the Sabbath. For then there will be great distress, unequaled from the beginning of the world until now— and never to be equaled again.*
>
> *"If those days had not been cut short, no one would survive, but for the sake of the elect those days will be shortened*
>
> *Matthew 24:14-22 (NIV)*

This describes brief disaster, not an enduring period of destruction that ends the world, but one in which some people survive. It is thus consistent with the expectation of a world without end.

By its very nature, the end of the world cannot be proven while the world still exists. Because the message is cryptic, different Christian groups speak of the end days or the world without end. People speculate about the identity of, and the way to recognize, "the abomination that causes desolation," that according to Matthew 24:15 will indicate the beginning of the end. Whatever the conclusion, it is not an issue that changes the prescriptions for our daily lives and how we should prepare and be ready for such an occurrence.

Reminiscent of the great flood (Genesis 6-7) which reported that Noah, his family and genetic bases of other species (Genesis 7:2-3) were spared, this account also reports that some would be saved (Matthew 22:22). Therefore, although it does describe a dreadful event of great distress, incomparable with anything previously experienced, the end does spare some remnant of life. In that sense, the world itself, through this remnant of survivors, is not placed out of existence by the catastrophe.

In this way, these strangely perplexing expectations of a world without end and of an expectation of end times become reconciled.

Christians hope for a world without end. Yet it is prudent to share concern for observations and projections such as global warming. Evidence of deserts and glaciers speak of other climactic changes that the world has survived. The planet is ours to care for (Genesis 1:26 and Genesis 2:15). However, as we face the prospect of global warming it is with the enlightened perspectives of the world without end.

In any event, the prophecies about end times do not change the fate of each of us, the expectation of life, death or eternal life. Our lives unfold within the context of the world, whatever its fate. Whatever that abomination that causes the desolation of the world, should it occur within our lifetimes, we have the hope of being among that remnant that will ensure the world without end.

Reflect and Explore:

A) Review these discussions and share with others.

B) What questions, if any, do you have for the author? You are invited to visit the book's website and share your reflections and questions.

Conclusions

There is no pressure on anyone to believe this. Tangible proof is perceived through the five senses that we popularly recognize: the witness of the eyes or ears, touching the proof or experience of taste and smell. When proof that God exists is recorded or reported, the rational person then seeks to validate it. Oftentimes then, as in assessing whether someone is telling the truth, the question becomes a matter of whether one believes the source. Like judges, we judge and make conclusions about belief.

How I know that God exists stems from my personal experience and from assessment of the evidence reported and recorded by others, primarily in the Bible. My understanding of Bible stories, my understanding about prayer, my sense of truth and falsehood, and the Spirit of Truth in me all influence that knowledge. Everyone's experience will not be the same as mine. However, understandings that I share may serve to help others along the way. In particular, placing scribes in perspective and appreciating what the Bible represents should help people overcome skepticism inspired by the way Christians are perceived today.

The understanding of what life is -- that it includes physical death and that a life well lived includes planes of existence other than the physical -- leads to the perception that the formal educational and information systems are constructed to support particular planes. All planes of existence are not equally supported by our societies and cultures, and educated people are left struggling to understand life and how to live beyond the confines of careers. Yet, we each are blessed with the Spirit of Truth that, once we are ready, can help us cross hurdles and boundaries of belief that make us wary and skeptical about the existence of God.

The discussions show that theories of evolution can be discredited on bases of the same sciences on which they are founded. Other (contradictory) conclusions can be drawn from the same evidence, many assumptions are presumed to be true and there are gaps and missing links needed to cement the hypotheses. Violating the same principles of science encompassing them, the discredit and disproof are legitimate and compelling, and grounds for open-minded readers' disbelief. In contrast, creation cannot rightly be discredited on bases of principles on which it is not founded, and it cannot be disproven in any forum. Simply put, the scientific theory of evolution does not withstand scientific testing and creation neither pretends to be science nor to apply courtroom standards of proof. Both evolution and creation are issues of belief. Creationists unpretentiously cite belief. Evolutionists do not. Given the demands of science, precise evolutionists looking at the evidence will eventually revise belief in evolution because of concrete inconsistencies with evidence of the human condition and inability to arrive at objectively verifiable conclusions.

By separating the essential truths of Christianity from the muddle of the many different ways that people and denominations of Christianity serve and worship God, the journey through skepticism can stay on the course of issues that are important. Disputes including the date of Jesus' birth, the correct day for Sabbath and the meaning of the creation story need not deter anyone seeking a relationship with God. There are unifying beliefs among Christians. The different denominations and varied perspectives open opportunities for each seeker in the diverse world population to find a suitable home to nurture the spirit as part of the universal body standing for Christ.

You need not fear jokes and taunts about belief when you understand what makes the jokes funny. You may also laugh at yourself and share in what must seem like incredulity regarding some beliefs, to those who observe only the rules of evidence acceptable in courts of law and deny their own knowledge and sense of truth. While it is customary to leave decisions about truth to appointed judges' opinions, truth exists beyond material evidence. Not every thing that is true is accompanied by tangible material. One cannot deny it may seem funny to trust an invisible God and an unacknowledged sense of the Spirit of Truth within us, until one does. It is laughable in a world that depends on sight. Seeing the humor is no denial of the truth. Indeed, it takes intelligence to *really* laugh. No one enjoys a joke better than those who understand *why* it is funny. Being funny in an audience that will not see does not invalidate God.

Distinguishing between Christian 'nice to have's' and Christian promises and hopes puts in perspective those misunderstandings that inevitably disappoint, and those Christian hopes, invisible and unseen, that await confirmation. Some things are misunderstood. Some promises await confirmation. Different denominations may interpret scriptures differently and follow what may appear to be conflicting practices and beliefs, but all fall short and seek the same God. What is inviolable despite variations in sacraments and rituals is Jesus' teaching that loving God and loving others is the most important aspect of our lives.

Nothing in the Bible is in conflict, although different interpretations may be. No interpretation is final. God's omniscience and omnipotence rise above our limited human perspectives.

We are able to conclude that Christians are not delusional, but hopeful. There is no contradiction between Christian life and reality. Life as a Christian takes understanding of what is real, what is true and what is *to be seen,* and the ability to distinguish these. We accept that we do not know nor perceive everything, and that some things are mystery. In other words, the quiet sense acknowledges our human limitations and does not deny reality.

Ultimately, death is the sleep that plagues wise and foolish alike, criminals and saints, believers and unbelievers, sheep and goats. Whatever will happen to us beyond death is unseen. We have free will and free choice before death to take the opportunities that life offers. In that circumstance as adults, it is our choice whether or not we recognize and nurture our spirits. We can choose to prepare for experience in another world or remain skeptical. Analysis may inspire skepticism, and it is respected. Informed analysis will incorporate all relevant dimensions. There is no *legal* proof, but spiritual knowledge and historical records. It is each individual's personal choice whether they want to live a full life on all planes.

In final analysis, it is proposed that the quiet sense rests in each of us. It is the Spirit of Truth, unlike the senses that we as a culture acknowledge. Some people recognize the Spirit of Truth and some don't. Some, though unaware, are nevertheless children of God. It is not in our power to select who is a child of God and who is not. The Shepherd will recognize his sheep. The explanations in this book are just that: explanations, not *legal* proof. At best, they could awaken the dormant and help those who stumble over barriers on contemporary roads.

The intent of this analysis is not to compel or exert pressure to believe one school or another. It explains selected Christian beliefs in the context of contemporary skepticism and unbelief and points readers to clearer understanding of them. The analysis informs, reasons and explains how I *know* that God is real. Free will is unbounded in its entirety. The unexplored quiet sense, the Spirit of Truth, will serve as a personal compass for each of us as we exercise that free will.

> *He who began a good work in you will carry it on to completion until the day of Christ Jesus*
>
> *Philippians 1:6 (NIV)*

END

References

Benson, Herbert, M.D. and Proctor, William, Your Maximum Mind, 1987, Random House of Canada, Inc., Toronto

Covey, Steven, The Seven Habits of Highly Effective People, 1989, Fireside, New York, NY

Darwin, Charles, The Origin of Species by Means of Natural Selection, or the preservation of favored races in the struggle for life, 1993, Random House, Inc. New York

de Bono, Edward, The Mechanism of Mind, 1969, Penguin Books Ltd., Middlesex, England

Dunbar, Paul Laurence, The complete poems of Paul Laurence Dunbar / with an introd. to "Lyrics of lowly life" by W. D. Howells, 1980, Dodd, Mead, New York

Haas, J.W., Jr., John Wesley's Vision of Science in the Service of Christ, 1984, Prospectives on Science and Christian Faith, 47

Hamilton, Adam, The Way, Walking in the Footsteps of Jesus, Abingdon Press, Nashville, TN

Johnson, Luke Timothy, The Creed: What Christians believe and why it matters, 2004, Doubleday, New York, NY

Lewis, C.S. Mere Christianity, 1952, C.S. Lewis Pte, Ltd., Harper Collins, audio Ed.

Sinclair, Karen, Jungle Heart, 1992, Barbados

Smith, Adam, An Inquiry into the Nature and Causes of the Wealth of Nations, 1776, public domain

Spong, Rev. John Shelby, Eternal Life: A New Vision, 2009, HarperOne, New York, NY

Warren, Rick, The Purpose Driven Life, 2012, Zondervan, Nashville, TN

Wesley, John, An Earnest Appeal to Men of Reason and Religion, 1813, Shaw & Shoemaker, New York

http://news.nationalgeographic.com/news/2009/05/090519-missing-link-found.html

http://www.nationalgeographic.org/news/who-was-ida/

http://news.nationalgeographic.com/news/2002/11/1120_021120_raptor.html

http://www.ideacenter.org/contentmgr/showdetails.php/id/1503

http://paulocoelhoblog.com/2007/12/10/the-lesson-of-the-butterfly/

http://www.theopedia.com/prayer

http://www.theopedia.com/salvation

http://internetbiblecollege.net/lessons/hebrew%20and%20greek%20words%20for%20forgiveness%20or%20pardon.htm

https://www.edge.org/conversation/j_craig_venter-what-is-life-a-21st-century-perspective

https://www.trinitywallstreet.org/video/justin-welby-opening-service

http://www.godrules.net/library/wesley/274wesley_h2.htm

http://www.biblegateway.com

http://www.etymonline.com

http://www.internetbiblecollege.net

http://www.lornasalzman.com

http://www.umc.org

Bibles

The Holy Bible, New International Version, (NIV) by Biblica, Inc.®

Holy Bible, New International Version® Anglicized, (NIVUK) by Biblica, Inc.

The Holy Bible, the New King James Version®, (NKJV) by Thomas Nelson

The Holy Bible, King James Version (KJV), public domain

The Holy Bible, New Living Translation (NLT), by Tyndale House Publishers, Inc.,

The Holy Bible, International Standard Version (ISV) by Davidson Press, LLC

Movies and Music

Scorsese, M., Winter, T., DiCaprio, L., Aziz, R., McFarland, J., Koskoff, E. T., Kacandes, G., ... EMJAG Productions, (2014), *The Wolf of Wall Street*.

Gibson, M., Fitzgerald, B., Davey, B., McEveety, S., Caviezel, J., Bellucci, M., Gerini, C., Twentieth Century Fox Home Entertainment, Inc., (2004), *The Passion of the Christ*.

John, Elton, Goodbye, England's Rose, Co-writer Bernie Taupin, 1997, Producer Sir George Martin

Keep Track of Your Favorite Bible Verses

NOTES

www.ingramcontent.com/pod-product-compliance
Lightning Source LLC
Chambersburg PA
CBHW032105090426
42743CB00007B/246